WHY WE DO WHAT WE DO

The Dynamics of Personal Autonomy

EDWARD L. DECI

WITH RICHARD FLASTE

A Grosset/Putnam Book
Published by G. P. Putnam's Sons • New York

A Grosset/Putnam Book
Published by G. P. Putnam's Sons
Publishers Since 1838
200 Madison Avenue
New York, NY 10016

Library of Congress Cataloging-in-Publication Data

Deci, Edward L.
   Why we do what we do : the dynamics of personal autonomy /
by Edward L. Deci with Richard Flaste.
      p.   cm.
   "A Grosset/Putnam book."
   Includes bibliographical references.
   ISBN 0-399-14047-6 (alk. paper)
   1. Autonomy (Psychology)   2. Motivation (Psychology)
I. Flaste, Richard. II. Title.
BF575.A88D45   1995   95-1901 CIP
153.8—dc20

Printed in the United States of America
Design by Ann Gold

10 9 8 7 6 5 4 3 2 1

This book is printed on acid-free paper.∞

ACKNOWLEDGMENTS

Most of all, I am grateful to Richard M. Ryan, with whom I have collaborated for nearly twenty years. Much of the research discussed in this book is more his than mine. He read multiple versions of the manuscript and made countless important inputs. Ryan and I have also had several other collaborators whose contributions have helped to make this book possible. I am grateful to all of them. Finally, Christopher Walsh, Jay Ryan, Betsy Whitehead, and Sebby Jacobson read a draft of the manuscript and made useful suggestions.

—E. L. D.

CONTENTS

WHY WE DO
WHAT WE DO

ONE

Authority and Its Discontents

S truggling to make their way among the stresses and pressures of life, many people have been pushed to the point of acting irresponsibly. They are alienated and disaffected, and it shows up in countless ways. Violence has become commonplace within families and out on the streets. Acting out is rampant in our schools. Insider trading and price fixing seem to be the norm. Obesity and anorexia are at near-epidemic proportions. And people face crippling debt.

Surely, individuals pay dearly for their irresponsibility, but so also do those closest to them. The irresponsibility of parents is costly to their children, and the irresponsibility of managers, doctors, and teachers is costly to their employees, patients, and students. By failing to deal effectively with the stresses and pressures in their own lives, individuals add stresses and pressures to the lives of others.

Many people today have had enough of this. They feel like the world is raging out of control, and they're fed up. They want to crack down, achieve discipline, make those around them behave better. They resonate to the writers and politicians who call for more accountability, who view the problems in terms of morality, who say it's time to tighten control.

Control is an easy answer. It assumes that the promise of reward or the threat of punishment will make the offenders comply. And it sounds tough, so it feels reassuring to people who believe things have gone awry but have neither the time nor the energy to think about the problems, let alone *do* something about them.

In spite of the appeal of control, however, it has become increasingly clear that the approach simply does not work. Attempts to apply stricter discipline have been largely ineffectual, and the widespread reliance on rewards and punishments to motivate responsibility has failed to yield the desired results. Indeed, mounting evidence suggests that these so-called solutions, based on the principle of rigid authority, are exacerbating rather than ameliorating the problems.

An alternative approach begins not with blame and control, but with asking why people are behaving irresponsibly in the first place—why they are being violent, engaging in unhealthy behaviors, going hopelessly into debt, or ignoring their children in order to amass a fortune. This approach takes the individuals' perspective, focuses on the motivation underlying their irresponsibility, and explicates the social forces that influence that motivation. It then addresses the factors that can lead people to behave more responsibly.

This book is about human motivation, and it is organized around the important distinction between whether a behavior is autonomous or controlled. Etymologically the term autonomy derives from being self-governing. To be autonomous means to act in accord with one's self—it means feeling free and volitional in one's actions. When autonomous, people are fully willing to do what they are doing, and they embrace the activity with a sense of interest and commitment. Their actions emanate from their true sense of self, so they are being authentic. In contrast, to be controlled means to act because one is being pressured. When controlled, people act without a sense of personal endorsement. Their behavior is not an expression of the self, for the self has been subjugated to the controls. In this condition, people can reasonably be described as alienated.

The issues of autonomy and authenticity, as opposed to control and alienation, are relevant in all aspects of life. They are sometimes manifest dramatically, with societal implications, and other times, subtly, with only personal ramifications.

A man who resists the pressures to succumb to price fixing because he personally believes it is wrong is acting autonomously and living authentically. But if he succumbs to the pressures, and in the process, brings serious harm to thousands and adds to the negative national tone, he is being controlled and inauthentic. A woman who serves on the school board with a full sense of volition because she believes in its importance is being autonomous and authentic. But if, in spite of not wanting to, she serves because she thinks it looks good to others, she too is being controlled and inauthentic.

To the extent that a behavior is not autonomous it is controlled, and there are two types of controlled behavior. The first type is compliance, and it is compliance that authoritarian solutions hope to accomplish. Compliance means doing what you are told to do because you are told to do it. I remember years ago when the television networks began the practice of following a Presidential address with the dissenting views of opposing senators or congressmen. A friend of mine remarked, "I don't think it's right for them to do that."

"What do you mean?" I replied. "Dissenting opinions deserve to be heard."

"But he's the President," my friend protested.

Although such reverence for the President seems almost quaint today, the comment epitomizes the compliant attitude. Noted author Charles Reich spoke about "the nameless authority." This was the authority firmly lodged in my friend's ideology, leading him to think and behave compliantly.

The other response to control is defiance, which means to do the opposite of what you are expected to do just because you are expected to do it. Compliance and defiance exist in an unstable partnership representing the complementary responses to control. Where there is one, there is also the tendency for the other, even though one or the other is typically dominant within an individual. Thus, we find some people who are highly compliant, always seeming to do what the situation demands, and we find others who seem to defy all the demands and prods of authorities. But even with these people, where one response to control dominates, the tendency for the other will still be there and could come out in subtle ways. A subordinate who is outwardly obedient to all the boss's demands might, for example, engage in secret sabotage as retaliation.

Rebellion is the outward manifestation of people's tendency to defy controls, and it coexists uneasily with conformity, which is the expression of their tendency to comply. Authoritarians of our era have relied on control, and they have gotten a healthy dose of rebellion along with the conformity they had hoped for. But what is even worse, and what has gone largely unrecognized, is that the price of compliance is itself very steep. That price—profound alienation with all of its ramifications—is detailed in this book.

A uthenticity necessitates behaving autonomously, for it means being the author of one's actions—acting in accord with one's true inner self. The key to understanding autonomy, authenticity, and self is the psychological process called integration. Various aspects of a person's psyche differ in the degree to which they have been integrated or brought into harmony with the person's innate, core self. Only when the processes that initiate and regulate an action are integrated aspects of one's self would the behavior be autonomous and the person, authentic. It is in this sense that to be authentic is to be true to one's self.

An obvious and important implication of our conception of self as the integrated center out of which one acts freely and volitionally is that it is possible, metaphorically, for the cause of an action to be within the person but not within the self. No one would say that psychotic behaviors are authentic or self-determined. They are initiated by some aspect of a person's psychic makeup, but they do not proceed from what we term the self. The serial killer "Son of Sam," for example, claimed to have heard voices telling him to murder.

Clearly, the voices came from within *him*, but they did not represent aspects of his *self*.

Less clear, but perhaps even more important, are common everyday instances in which people have internalized rigid controls from society and respond compliantly to those forces within them. Such behaviors lack the qualities of freedom and flexibility that characterize autonomy and authenticity. Think about the man who goes to church not because he wants to but because he thinks he should. He is being neither autonomous nor authentic when he behaves with the experience of "having to" rather than "choosing to."

There are also instances where people defy internal pressures. Think about the young woman who internalizes her parents' demands to become a physician, and then pressures herself to take premed courses in college. Not doing well, because her self is not in it, she eventually defies the pressures by dropping out of school altogether. In spite of enjoying learning about some subjects, she drops out because she is no longer willing to submit to the internal controls. She is being neither autonomous nor authentic in her act of defiance.

Because integration is a defining aspect of self, it is quite possible for behavior to be initiated and regulated by aspects of a person that are alien to the self. Taking account of such alien aspects is necessary for gaining an understanding of autonomy versus control, and of the rebellion, conformity, and "self-indulgence" that one observes every day. It is also necessary for understanding a variety of other manifestations of alienation and inauthenticity—behaviors such as spousal abuse and the battered wife syndrome, for example.

When one understands self to be the integrated, psychological core from which a person acts authentically, with true volition, it is easy to see why so much confusion has resulted from the writings of scholarly social critics such as Christopher Lasch and Allan Bloom who claim that authenticity spawns irresponsibility. For them, self—the "author" from which authenticity emanates—is essentially equated with person, so a focus on any aspect of a person is said to be absorption with the self.

Lasch, for example, describes American culture as having a narcissistic preoccupation with the self. He might be right about a narcissistic preoccupation in this culture, but it is not a preoccupation with the *self*. On the contrary, narcissism involves desperately seeking affirmation from *others*. It entails an outward focus—a concern with what others think—and that focus takes people away from their true self. The narcissistic preoccupation results not from people's being aligned with the self but from their having lost contact with it. They adopt narcissistic values in a controlling society because they have not had the type of psychological nourishment they need to develop an integrated and healthy self. Narcissism is not the result of authenticity or self-determination, it is their antithesis.

There is another vein of confusion that runs through the discussions of self presented by many psychologists and social critics. It concerns the relation of freedom or autonomy to independence or aloneness. This confusion is evident in Bloom's description of authenticity as people caring about themselves rather than others, and in the comment by historian Loren Baritz that when people are free, they are radically alone and lacking in emotional warmth. These views come out of the misconception that when people come into fuller contact with themselves, when they become freer in their functioning, when they unhook themselves from society's controls, they will opt for isolation over connectedness. But there is no evidence for that. Quite the contrary, as people become more authentic, as they develop greater capacity for autonomous self-regulation, they also become capable of a deeper relatedness to others.

It should be clear that authenticity cannot be understood in terms of outward behaviors alone; one must look to the motivations that underlie them. Some of the people who marched for civil rights in the sixties were being authentic; others were not. Some of the people who hang around health clubs in the nineties are being authentic; others are not. It is only by considering people's motivation for behaving—for going to church, doing their homework, dieting, having children, or, for that matter, stealing a loaf of bread—and examining the extent to which it is autonomous that we can address issues of authenticity, and ultimately, of responsibility.

For over twenty-five years I have been exploring the concepts of autonomy, authenticity, freedom, and true self, anchoring the exploration in motivational concepts. That work, which will be drawn upon in this book, has been done largely in collaboration with Richard Ryan. The work itself is presented in scientific form elsewhere, but in this book I use the work to address some fundamental issues related to the self in a social world.

Ryan and I are not the only psychologists who have been concerned with issues like autonomy and authenticity. Psychoanalytic writers Donald Winnicott and Alice Miller, for example, have also developed theories that emphasize the concept of true self. But their work has been done within a tradition that relies on therapeutic case material to provide the substance for theory development, whereas our work has been conducted within the so-called empirical tradition, which relies on the application of statistical principles to data gathered using scientific methods.

In using the empirical approach, we have employed concepts that are applicable to people's everyday lives, as they go to work or school, as they raise children and deal with the demands of their home lives, as they face challenges and make policies. Thus, by conceptualizing authenticity in terms of behaving autonomously, it becomes a specifiable quality of human functioning, rather than just an abstract philosophical concept. That has allowed it to be moved from the realm of reasoned speculation into the realm of psychological research. It has also given people a tool for reflecting on the extent to which they are being authentic in their own lives. Similarly, the concept of alienation, which philosophically means to be separate from one's self, can also be investigated and explained concretely in terms of behaviors that are pressured and controlled. The dozens of psychological investigations we have done have given palpable meaning to these concepts.

A ll of us find ourselves in a variety of relationships with differen-
tials in status, power, or control—relationships which have a
structure that might be referred to as one-up/one-down. These include relationships between parents and children, managers and
subordinates, teachers and students, doctors and patients. In these
relationships, one party—the parent, manager, teacher, or doctor—
can be understood as a socializing agent. As such, that person has the
job of facilitating motivation and responsibility in the other. In a
sense, these roles make people the embodiment of society and confer
on them the task of transmitting its values and mores. These relationships thus play a central role in the conceptions of autonomy and
control—and of authenticity and alienation—that are presented in
this book.

Most adults—as parents, community organizers, coaches, work-
group leaders, or health-care providers—are in positions where they
dispense advice and make demands. But they are also, at times, on
the receiving end. Even billionaire corporate CEOs have to follow
the orders of their physicians or spouses from time to time—as well
as the echoes of their parents' admonitions that also serve to control
them. People never cease struggling to find their own voice and direction amidst the forces that operate on them in their various roles
where others have authority over them.

Even intimate relationships—and others where people are osten-
sibly equal—are permeated by issues of autonomy and control. In
those relationships, however, there exists a daunting complexity in
which each partner not only struggles to be autonomous but also
needs to support the autonomy of the other. It is a delicate balance
between feeling free and supporting another's freedom, and it is a
dynamic that exemplifies how the issue of human autonomy is
woven through the texture of all connectedness among people.

To become more autonomous and authentic, people must come
to grips with their one-up/one-down relationships. In a sense, they
must transcend them. An examination of these relationships is particularly instructive because it highlights how people in positions of

authority—who are pivotal in creating what we call the social context of the people over whom they have authority—can affect the motivation of those people. It also reveals the strategies and needs of people in one-down positions as they strive to maintain and nurture their vitality for life. It is easy to find employees who feel like "slaves," but it is harder to find active workers who, in a meaningful sense, are their own masters. And not all managers help them. It is easy to find children who feel like part of "the crew," but it is harder to find ones who feel like the captains of their own ship. And not all parents and teachers help them. These are the kinds of issues that are relevant to fostering the motivation of people in one-down positions and, more broadly, to promoting human autonomy and responsibility within society.

M ost people seem to think that the most effective motivation comes from outside the person, that it is something one skillful person does to another. There are numerous prototypes. Think for example of the locker-room speech where the coach, through the power of his gifted tongue, coddles and urges, shames and exhorts, and in so doing turns wimps into champs. Or think of the orderly classroom where the concerned teacher, through the cunning use of rewards and punishments, turns little beasts into compliant learners.

To the contrary, however, all the work that Ryan and I have done indicates that *self*-motivation, rather than external motivation, is at the heart of creativity, responsibility, healthy behavior, and lasting change. External cunning or pressure (and their internalized counterparts) can sometimes bring about compliance, but with compliance come various negative consequences, including the urge to defy. Because neither compliance nor defiance exemplifies autonomy and authenticity, we have continuously had to confront an extremely important—seemingly paradoxical—question: How can people in one-up positions, such as health-care providers or teachers, motivate others, such as their patients or students, who are in one-down positions, if the most powerful motivation, leading to the most responsible behavior, must come from within—if it must be internal to the self of the people in the one-down positions?

In fact, the answer to this important question can be provided only when the question is reformulated. The proper question is not, "how can people motivate others?" but rather, *"how can people create the conditions within which others will motivate themselves?"* When we formulated the question in this way our investigations repeatedly confirmed that the orientations and actions of people in positions of authority do play an important role in determining whether those whom they supervise, teach, or care for will effectively motivate themselves—and, in fact, whether they will develop greater autonomy and authenticity. This book lays out the way these social forces operate to affect motivation and development.

Throughout life people grapple with the issue of whether they are making their own choices—whether their actions are self-determined or, alternatively, are controlled by an external agent or by some powerful force within them. Choice is the key to self-determination and authenticity, and the question of whether someone really chooses to do something is essential to most civil and criminal trials. Millions of dollars may be decided over the issue of whether a patient really did give informed consent to a medical procedure. And the decision between the death sentence and incarceration in a psychiatric hospital may depend on a jury's answer to whether the gunman *chose* to pull the trigger or was forced by some internal urge that could be labeled "temporary insanity."

The issue for society concerns the conditions—both actual and psychological—under which people should be held accountable for their actions. And of course some lawyers have picked up on this and worked to push the balance one way or the other. In the most extreme modern development, the criminal justice system has toyed with the concept of "imperfect self-defense" in which, for example, Lorena Bobbitt or the Menendez brothers do not deny that they committed terrible acts, but maintain that the commission of these acts was not volitional, that they were driven by a personal environment so painful that they saw no alternative. They aggressed as a self-defense even though they were not under immediate attack. They acted with grotesque violence, it is argued, because they *believed* they had to.

Complex and fascinating as the issues of autonomy and authenticity may be when considered at the level of cultures or interpersonal relationships, they become even richer and more stimulating when viewed solely within the individual. A master-slave relationship exists to some extent within everyone. People can regulate themselves in quite autonomous and authentic ways, or alternatively in quite controlling and dictatorial ways, pressuring and criticizing themselves. The extent to which it is one versus the other depends on the degree of resolution of that master-slave dichotomy.

Many people find this idea easy to comprehend in the case of, say, an addict, who is a slave to her addiction, or of an obsessive-compulsive, who is a slave to his compulsions. But the dynamics are just as relevant for many other behaviors. The dynamics begin as interpersonal processes in the home, at school, and elsewhere, and are taken in by people in ways that are more healthy, or less. Understanding these processes—the intrapsychic processes as well as the interpersonal ones—allows meaningful answers to important questions. It is an understanding that can help people maintain smoking cessation, nurture an unflagging interest in learning, and perform well in sports. It is also an understanding that is essential for locating and anchoring one's true self amidst the seductive and coercive tides of modern culture.

The aims of this book are simply stated: They are to use a comprehensive body of motivational research to examine the relation between autonomy and responsibility and to reflect on the issue of promoting responsibility in an alienating world. The book is full of hope, for it speaks to what we can do for ourselves, and what we can do for our children, our employees, our patients, our students, and our athletes—indeed, what we can do for our society. The prescriptions it offers are not panaceas, and they are not easy. But they are relevant to each of us in managing ourselves, and they apply to the roles of teacher, manager, parent, doctor, and coach. Indeed, they are relevant and important for everyone in policy-making positions. The prescriptions begin with an understanding of people's motivation—of the extent to which it is autonomous—and they involve using that understanding to manage ourselves more effectively, to relate differently to others, and to make more meaningful social policy.

Like the works by Lasch, Bloom, Baritz, and others, this book decries much of the state of things: The insidiousness of advertising that hooks people's egos; the way people in dominating positions control and demean the people with whom they interact; the incredible emphasis on instrumental thinking (of seeing everything as a means to an end); the overvaluing of material possessions; and the erosion of community giving. But in this book, social criticism is secondary; it is more implicit than explicit. What is primary is a delineation of the processes through which society's fragmentation affects the lives of its members and a consideration of what can be done about it.

In studying authenticity and alienation, Ryan and I have used scientific methods to explore their motivational bases. These methods were developed largely by people who believed in what Aristotle called the efficient causation of behavior, which essentially means that antecedent events force one to behave. But there is no reason why the methods cannot be applied to the study of concepts like psychological freedom that had previously been addressed primarily by humanists and philosophers without the aid of scientific methods.

Although use of the empirical approach has the great advantage of allowing confirmation or disconfirmation of theoretical hypotheses, it also has a substantial disadvantage: It is an enormously slow and methodical process. For more than a quarter century, the results of dozens of experiments and field studies—performed in the psychology laboratory as well as in homes, business, schools, and clinics in this country and abroad—have accumulated. In this book, I use the results of those studies as a basis for discussing human freedom and responsibility. As such, the social criticisms and prescriptions contained herein represent extrapolations and speculations. What began as statistical inferences from systematic observations is here used to shed light on broad human problems.

Our study of personal autonomy—of authenticity and responsibility—has focused on motivational processes. By examining behaviors that can be properly described as autonomous and exploring the motivational processes through which they are regulated, we have been able to detail both the social-contextual antecedents of these behaviors and their consequences. These matters are at the heart of this book. They speak to why we do what we do, and they provide a basis for addressing concrete and practical questions such as how to promote responsible behaviors—like effective work performance, efficient and enjoyable learning, and long-term healthy behavior change—that benefit society as well as its individuals.

PART ONE

The Importance of Autonomy and Competence

TWO

I'm Only in It for the Money

Early Experiments on Rewards and Alienation

Visit any urban zoo, even a very progressive one, and you may well witness the familiar seal act. At the Prospect Park Zoo in Brooklyn, for instance, the young feeders enter the seal area at a designated hour, carrying their bags of fish, and proceed to create a spectacle that delights the youngsters and their parents who are crushed up against the fence watching. The feeders are not there as ringmasters to provide entertainment, but doing their job inevitably yields the bonus of a good show. As they drop each fish into the mouth of a ravenous seal, the seal will do almost anything to keep the supply coming. Clap their flippers together; wave to the crowd; arch their bodies like mermaids in a fountain. It's all there, and the spectators love it.

These feeders are extremely effective in the use of rewards to elicit desired behaviors, and such spectacles seem to attest to the power of rewards as a preeminent motivational technique. "If it works that well with the seals," a person might think, "it ought also to work with my children, and with my students and employees." The message seems simple: Reward the desired behavior, and there is increased likelihood that the behavior will be repeated.

As it turns out, the issue is really not so simple. And you can get a glimpse of the problem even with the seals. Just as soon as the feeders disappear, so too do the entertaining behaviors. The seals no longer have interest in clapping their flippers together or waving to the crowd. Rewards may increase the likelihood of behaviors, but only so long as the rewards keep coming.

With our children, students, and employees we typically hope that the desired behaviors will continue even if we are not there to toss them a fish. We'd like them to keep learning, to keep producing, to keep doing their share of housework, and the question we face is how to promote such persistent self-direction rather than the irresponsibility or alienation that seems so prevalent in today's world. It is a big question indeed, and formulating the answer begins with an interesting concept from the work of Harry Harlow, a pioneering psychologist who spent most of his career studying rhesus monkeys.

Monkeys are an energetic lot, frequently engaged in all manner of playful antics. They run around, poke each other, throw things, make faces, and seem to have a very good time. But not all of their energy and attention goes to idle play. Harlow placed monkeys, one at a time, in a cage that contained a kind of puzzle apparatus—a series of hasps, hooks, and hinges. The monkeys took great interest in this mechanical puzzle. They would figure out how to open it; then how to close it up again. And they would repeat their actions many times. There were no tangible rewards for the behavior, and yet these naturally inquisitive monkeys were focused and determined. What's more, they seemed to be enjoying themselves. Harlow used the term intrinsic motivation to explain why the monkeys had spent many hours working on the puzzles, where the only possible "reward" seemed to be the activity itself.

Although it's important not to go too far with animal-human comparisons, the spontaneous, though clearly constructive, behavior of those monkeys inspires one to think about similar behaviors in young children. A child's curiosity is an astonishing source of energy. Children explore, manipulate, and question; they pick things up, shake them, taste them, throw them, and ask, "What's this?" Every bit as interested in a cardboard box as in a gleaming new plastic marvel, they try things, bend things, and transform one thing into another. They seek the novel and they are eager to learn. Clearly, something in them is alive and vital; something in them wants to master the challenges of their lives. The term intrinsic motivation seems to apply just as well to these children as it did to Harlow's monkeys.

For young children, learning is a primary occupation; it is what they do naturally and with considerable intensity when they are not preoccupied with satisfying their hunger or dealing with their parents' demands. But one of the most troubling problems we face in this culture is that as children grow older they suffer a profound loss. In schools, for example, they seem to display so little of the natural curiosity and excitement about learning that was patently evident in those very same children when they were three or four years old. What has happened? Why is it that so many of today's students are unmotivated, when it could not be more clear that they were born with a natural desire to learn? It was this disturbing issue that prompted me to begin studying motivation in an attempt to understand more about the interplay of authenticity and the social world. After all, what could be more authentic than the curiosity and vitality of a normal three-year-old?

In the early 1960s, I had started studying psychology as an undergraduate at Hamilton College in Clinton, New York. It was the alma mater of B. F. Skinner, the renowned behaviorist whose pioneering work had led to the development of behavior modification programs and the systematic use of rewards—or, in the vernacular of behaviorism, reinforcements. At Hamilton, I was steeped in the principles of behaviorism: Deliver a reward for a specific, identifiable behavior and do so as soon after the behavior as possible; focus on rewards rather than punishments; and be consistent in delivering the rewards. These, of course, are precisely the principles that worked so well with the seals in Prospect Park.

The principles of behaviorism appeal to many psychologists and laymen alike; they fit philosophically with the general idea that striving for rewards—for financial success in particular—is the American way. They also fit with the increasing call for more control within society, and with the view taken by so many educators that the way to get students to learn is through the use of grades, gold stars, and other rewards. Tell them what they should do and then reward them for complying. The answer to how to motivate children's learning, in this view, is quite straightforward: Use the appropriate reward contingencies.

Although the fine points of the behavioral approach are somewhat complex, its message, as behaviorist philosopher Barry Schwartz pointed out, is rather simple: People are fundamentally passive and will respond only when the environment tempts them with the opportunity to get rewards or avoid punishments.

In 1969, as a doctoral student in psychology at Carnegie-Mellon University in Pittsburgh, I became increasingly captivated by the question of what happens to people's curiosity and vitality over time. Although I had first formulated the question with respect to children's learning, the more I thought about it the more I realized that the question has relevance in many other domains as well. The behaviorist's answer to the question would be that any lack of motivation could be attributed to inadequate reward contingencies, but I found that answer noncompelling, even disturbing.

Behaviorist dogma assumes that there is no inherent motivation to learn, but this does not square with the fact that young children— in preschools and at home—ceaselessly explore and manipulate the objects they encounter. They challenge themselves to become competent, apparently just for the enjoyment of doing it. Children are not passively waiting to be drawn into learning by the offer of rewards but rather are actively engaged in the process of learning. Indeed, they are *intrinsically motivated* to learn.

The behaviorist's assumption that there is no inherent motivation may seem to have validity in that many people act unmotivated. In a variety of life situations, for example, people can be found doing as little as they can get away with. Even in schools, many children are passive, lacking the interest and excitement for learning that seems so natural in three-year-olds. That, of course, was the very discrepancy that left me wondering about intrinsic motivation and what happens to it over time.

My doubting the behaviorists' dogma only added to my resolve

that the questions so many people ask—namely, "How
people to learn? to work? to do their chores? or to ta
cine?"—are the wrong questions. They are wrong
imply that motivation is something that gets done to p̲e̲o̲p̲l̲e̲ ̲...
than something that people do. A more fundamental and useful way
to think about the issue involves accepting the concept of intrinsic
motivation, which refers to the process of doing an activity for its
own sake, of doing an activity for the reward that is inherent in the
activity itself. Intrinsic motivation describes perfectly the learning
behavior of young children, and it also seems to have relevance to the
behavior of all of us who engage in a variety of activities (like leisure
pursuits) simply for the feelings of excitement, accomplishment, and
personal satisfaction they yield. Thinking about this concept then
leads one to ask the question of what kinds of experiences affect
people's intrinsic motivation, often leading to its being undermined.

Robert Henri, perhaps the greatest American art teacher of the
twentieth century, once captured the essence of being intrinsically
motivated when he wrote: "The object of painting a picture is not to
make a picture—however unreasonable this may sound. The picture,
if a picture results, is a by-product and may be useful, valuable, interesting as a sign of what has passed. The object, which is back of every
true work of art, is *the attainment of a state of being,* a high state of
functioning, a more than ordinary moment of existence." Henri's
point, quite simply, is that being intrinsically motivated has to do
with being wholly involved in the activity itself and not with reaching a goal (whether the goal be making money or making a picture).

Most of the learning of preschool children is done not because it
is instrumental for achieving something else, but because the children are curious, because they want to know. Clearly, their learning
is intrinsically motivated, and their intense involvement with learning represents a prototype of the "more than ordinary moment of
existence."

Although the idea of intrinsic motivation for learning seems to
capture the truth of, say, preschool children's activity, the seeming
fragility of this intrinsic motivation is quite haunting. And this seem-

ing fragility, of course, relates directly to the question of why there is not more intrinsic motivation for learning in older children. In thinking about it back in 1969, I had the fleeting—and surely blasphemous—thought that maybe all the rewards, rules, and regimentation that were so widely used to motivate schoolchildren were themselves the villains, promoting not an excited state of learning but a sad state of apathy.

Impelled by the possibility that I was onto something, I was finally able to formulate my question in a way so I could run an experiment to answer it. The question was this: "What happens to people's intrinsic motivation for an activity when they receive an extrinsic reward for doing the activity that they had previously been quite willing to do without the reward?" I decided to use a monetary payment as the reward to start what would turn into a major research program.

An appealing aspect of this inquiry, from the point of view of psychological science, was that I really had no idea if my suspicion about the deleterious effects of rewards was on the mark. Clearly, the dominant academic "wisdom" of the time was that the exact opposite would be true. Maybe intrinsic motivation and extrinsic rewards would combine in a positive and productive way, rather than a negative, antagonistic way. Maybe, for example, when people get an extrinsic reward for doing something they find intrinsically interesting, they enjoy the experience even more and want to keep doing it. If that turned out to be true, I would have to look for a different avenue into the issue of why so many students are not motivated to learn.

With the help of Victor Vroom, my mentor at Carnegie-Mellon, I developed a general research design—what is called an experimental paradigm—for exploring the question of how rewards affect intrinsic motivation. The work would take place in the psychological laboratory, which is a small, neutral room with few adornments where everything that happens can be controlled or manipulated by an experimenter. It's an artificial environment, of course, but we psychologists believe it provides the possibility for understanding the real world through analogy. If we can make something happen in the lab, using stimuli (called independent variables) that occur in day-to-day life, we assume that the same phenomenon probably also occurs out there in the real world. The advantage of a lab is that it allows us to ask very specific questions and observe relatively definitive answers. Eventually, if we find interesting results in the lab, we can venture into the field—that is, into schools, homes, workplaces, and clinics—to see if the findings hold up there.

To do the experiment, I needed an experimental task, something that the college student subjects would surely find intrinsically motivating. Fortuitously, I wandered into the office of a fellow graduate student one day and discovered a set of oddly shaped blocks, a puzzle called Soma, just produced by Parker Brothers. "The World's Finest Cube Puzzle Game" is how it was described on the instruction booklet. The puzzle had seven pieces, each shaped differently, and when fitted together in a particular way, the pieces formed a three-inch cube. In addition, there were thousands of different ways the pieces could be assembled to form various patterns. One such pattern shown in the booklet was called "Sam's Sitting Dog," another, "The Couch," a third, "The Airplane," and so on. Two of the seven pieces and the pattern for the sitting dog are shown on the next page.

Some of the shapes were easy, others were very difficult. The fun came in using the various pieces to reproduce the designs, and when that happened the feeling of accomplishment was quite palpable. Once someone gets started with the puzzles, it is tough to stop. I immediately found myself in the puzzles' thrall, completing one design after another. In fact, I started solving them in my mind. It seems that once you become familiar enough with them, you can actually assemble them in imaginary space even though on first encounter they may seem nearly impossible.

Soma was perfect because it allowed so much flexibility for experimental purposes: The same pieces could form many different designs; the difficulty level could be varied as needed; and impossible ones could be made to look easy. But most important, of course, they were challenging and interesting, and pilot testing demonstrated that

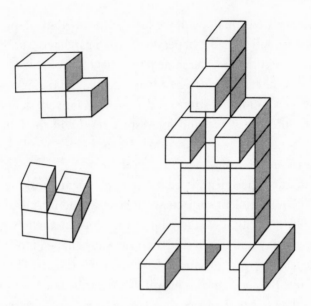

students loved them and would do them just for fun. In the experiment, subjects were shown several configurations that had been drawn on sheets of paper, and they were asked to try to reproduce the designs, in three-dimensional space, using the actual puzzle pieces.

The paradigm called for two groups of subjects: one group would receive extrinsic rewards for solving the puzzles (a buck apiece—and a buck was still worth something in 1969), and the second group would receive no rewards. The central question was: What will happen to the intrinsic motivation of the rewarded subjects relative to that of the nonrewarded subjects? Will it increase while working on the puzzles for pay, will it remain unchanged, or will it decrease?

Measuring the subjects' intrinsic motivation turned out to be a tricky matter. Here's how it was done: During the experiment, subjects sat at a table working intently on the Soma puzzle for half an hour or so. Then, the experimenter would tell them the puzzle-solving session was over, that he had to leave the room for a few minutes to enter their data in the computer and let the computer print out a questionnaire for them to complete. In actuality, the experimenter always departed for exactly eight minutes, and an essential part of the experiment concerned what the subjects did during that time. On the table near the students, there were some magazines intended to capture a variety of interests: *The New Yorker, Time,* and so on. During their time alone, the students could continue with the puzzles, read a magazine, or, I suppose, daydream. After the eight minutes had elapsed the experimenter returned with the questionnaire.

The most important period in this experiment wasn't the time the experimenter spent in the room, but the time he spent out of it. It was those eight minutes when the subjects could do as they pleased, waiting for the experimenter to return. As they waited, they were secretly observed to determine how much of the eight minutes of free-choice time they spent playing with the puzzles. The idea was that if they spent their free-choice time playing with the Soma, when no rewards would be forthcoming and when there were interesting alternative activities, then they must have been intrinsically motivated for the puzzles.

As it turned out, those students who had been rewarded monetarily for doing the puzzles were far less likely to play with them "just for fun" in the free-choice period. Stop the pay, and stop the play. It seems that once having been paid, these subjects were only in it for the money. And that was with an activity they had initially been quite willing to do without rewards. Introducing monetary rewards seems quickly to have made students dependent on those rewards, shifting their view of the puzzle from a satisfying activity in its own right to an activity that is instrumental for obtaining rewards. Unsettling though this finding may have been, from a scientific perspective it was very encouraging. Something important seemed to be emerging.

In a follow-up, I worked with the same general paradigm, but I took it into the field. I persuaded the editor of the school newspaper to put me in charge of headline writing so I could take an interesting activity students had been doing for free and start paying some of them for doing it. Then I could measure their continuing motivation

y, the funds had all dried up. Happily for me, this field
owed results comparable to those from the Soma-puz-
ce people started getting paid, they lost interest in the
, when the rewards stopped, they did not perform as
well.

One day I excitedly told a friend about the experiments, and a
few days later he gave me an old Jewish fable. The fable went something like this:

*It seems that bigots were eager to rid their town of a Jewish man
who had opened a tailor shop on Main Street, so they sent a group of
rowdies to harass the tailor. Each day, the ruffians would show up to
jeer. The situation was grim, but the tailor was ingenious. One day
when the hoodlums arrived, he gave each of them a dime for their
efforts. Delighted, they shouted their insults and moved on. The next
day they returned to shout, expecting their dime. But the tailor said
he could afford only a nickel and proceeded to hand a nickel to each
of them. Well, they were a bit disappointed, but a nickel is after all a
nickel, so they took it, did their jeering, and left. The next day, they
returned once again, and the tailor said he had only a penny for them
and held out his hand. Indignant, the young toughs sneered and proclaimed that they would certainly not spend their time jeering at him
for a measly penny. So they didn't. And all was well for the tailor.*

In doing research, it is important to remember that experimental
findings are always vulnerable to refutation, no matter how perfectly
devised and executed the experiment and no matter how persuasive
the results. So any time someone finds a new, counterintuitive, or
controversial result it is a good idea to try to obtain the result again.
After all, in using the methods of statistical inference to reach a con-
clusion about people in general from a small sample of them there is
always a small possibility of coming up with the wrong answer, just
by chance, if nothing else. After I moved to the University of Rochester, I replicated the study and found the same results: Monetary rewards undermined people's intrinsic motivation.

This finding, of course, did not go down easily in some quarters
of research psychology. After all, the assertion that monetary re-

wards can be counterproductive was almost brazenly iconoclastic. Neither was the position met with open arms by many people outside psychology. Indeed, even as investigators at other universities replicated and extended my results using other rewards (prizes, good-player awards, and food treats) and other-aged subjects (preschool children and high school students), sharp critiques began to appear in various journals and periodicals.

O bviously, money constitutes a powerful force. Certainly there can be no doubt that it motivates. One need only look around (even at oneself) to see how willing people are to engage in a wide range of activities for money. They drag themselves to work at jobs they hate, because they need the money. They get hooked on gambling, sometimes losing everything they own, because of the irrational belief that they will hit the big one. They take on extra assignments that unduly stress them, perhaps to the point of making them sick, because of the extra money. And they engage in a wide variety of nefarious activities that promise handsome rewards. Sure, money motivates, but that's not the point. The point is that while money is motivating people, it is also undermining their *intrinsic* motivation and, as we would later discover, having a variety of other negative effects as well.

In 1968, psychological theoretician Richard deCharms had published a book discussing the importance of a concept he called personal causation. He believed that the key to intrinsic motivation is the desire to be the "origin" of one's own action rather than a "pawn" manipulated by external forces. Using his line of thinking, the experiments seemed to suggest that rewards had undermined subjects' feelings of personal causation, and thus their intrinsic desire for mastery. Rewards seemed to turn the act of playing into something that was controlled from the outside: It turned play into work, and the player into a pawn.

Let's assume for a moment that these experiments have indeed isolated an important phenomenon and consider how these experimental results are pertinent to the kinds of issues raised in the first chapter. Of course you could appropriately take exception to my extrapolating from a few simple experiments conducted in the psychology laboratory to speak about such problems, but let's leave that objection aside for the moment because in time many other studies were done in many different settings that would buttress these results.

The experiments had shown that when subjects began getting paid for working on interesting puzzles, they lost interest. Although they would continue to do the puzzles for money—as so many people continue to do all manner of activities for money—their relation to the activity had become strained and instrumental. Think about it. A strained, instrumental relationship to an activity is a sure sign of the state called alienation. I had, in essence, promoted alienation in these subjects during a short and seemingly innocuous experiment. If that could be so, what must money be doing to people in the real world where it exerts so much power?

People today work long hours. According to the Economic Policy Institute, the average work year is now 158 hours longer than it was when this first intrinsic motivation experiment was performed. An extra month has been tacked on to what in 1969 was considered a full-time job! It is extraordinary really. Imagine that a king were to tell his subjects that they had to start working an additional 158 hours each year. Surely there would be a palace coup unless his army was very strong. But that increase has in fact happened in our society in a relatively short time, and no coup has occurred. Indeed, there has been barely an objection; only further alienation.

The power that has brought this about is not coercion—it is not a king's army—it is the seductive capacity of the regal dollar, along with the socialization processes within our society that keep the dollar enthroned. Money is indeed a seducer, and it seems to be closely related to the nameless authority that Charles Reich spoke about. When, for a short time during the sixties, large numbers of people rebelled against the traditional authority, the power of money seemed greatly diminished. But that era has passed, and the expanded work year has brought with it countless stresses and real costs to the individual.

Our experiments provide a scientific means of beginning to detail those costs quite specifically. The first cost is that people lose interest in many of the activities they perform. They begin to see the activities merely as instruments for attainment of monetary rewards, so they lose the excitement and vitality they once had for the activities. In an important sense, this finding is consistent with the idea that the people are losing contact with their inner selves when they become controlled by monetary rewards. Thus, these simple experiments may have begun to point to a profound phenomenon at the nexus between the inner person and the proddings of society.

When people talk about control, they usually mean coercion—they mean controlling through power and threats. Most people find it easy to accept that the use of force can have a range of negative consequences. Dictators control, and dictators are despised. But money also controls. When people say that money motivates, what they really mean is that money controls. And when it does, people become alienated—they give up some of their authenticity—and they push themselves to do what they think they must do. One take on the meaning of alienation is that it begins as people lose touch with their intrinsic motivation, with the vitality and excitement that all children possess, with the doing of an activity for its own sake, with the state of being that Robert Henri called a more than ordinary moment of existence.

THREE

The Need for Personal Autonomy

Although the early experiments had highlighted some negative consequences to the use of rewards as a motivator, the research had barely begun, for there were countless questions remaining to be addressed by carefully designed laboratory experiments and field studies.

To proceed, however, a fuller theoretical account of what had happened in the reward experiments was necessary so it could be used for deriving further hypotheses. Why might it be that people's intrinsic motivation—the vitality, spontaneity, genuineness, and curiosity that is intrinsic to people's nature—could be undermined by extrinsic rewards?

DeCharms's idea that people strive for personal causation—that they strive to feel like an origin of their own behavior—was a start, and the contributions of others like personality psychologist Henry Murray helped to fill out the conceptual picture. Murray had suggested that people have *needs* of the mind as well as needs of the body. Perhaps there is an innate or *intrinsic* need to feel a sense of personal autonomy or self-determination—to feel a sense of what deCharms had called personal causation. That would imply that people need to feel that their behavior is truly chosen by them rather than imposed by some external source—that the locus of initiation of their behavior is within themselves rather than in some external control. This is a rather subtle point, but its significance is quite profound. The implication of people having a need to feel autonomous is that failure to satisfy the need, like failure to satisfy the hunger need, could lead to decreased well-being—to a variety of maladaptive consequences.

The hypothesis, then, is that any occurrence that undermines people's feeling of autonomy—that leaves them feeling controlled—should decrease their intrinsic motivation and very likely have other negative consequences. The next step in the research program became quite clear: It was necessary to determine what other events or circumstances might decrease intrinsic motivation. In other words, what events, beyond rewards, are likely to be perceived by people as *controlling*—as limiting their autonomy?

One likely candidate, one widely used motivator that must surely be felt as controlling, was threat. People threaten others all the time—if you don't study you can't watch television; if you don't get to work on time you will be fired—and they assume that it's an effective motivational strategy. A threat, of course, is not intended to punish but instead is meant to motivate people through their desire to avoid a punishment.

Using the same general Soma paradigm as in the money experiments, we motivated puzzle solving by threatening to punish subjects if they failed to perform well. They did do well enough that they did not get punished, but the experience was a negative one nonetheless. In fact, threat worked much like money; it encouraged them to try to solve the puzzles, but it robbed them of the desire to engage in this playful activity for its own sake.

Other researchers, such as Mark Lepper and his colleagues at Stanford University, added to the list of events that yield similar negative consequences. Deadlines, imposed goals, surveillance, and evaluations were all found to undermine intrinsic motivation. That, of course, made sense because they all represent frequently used strategies for pressuring and controlling people. People experience them as being antagonistic to their autonomy, so these events drain people's sense of enthusiasm and interest in the controlled activities.

In one of the first seminars I taught at the University of Rochester, a student raised the issue of competition. Competition is certainly one of the mainstays of American culture. Tens of millions of people crowd around TV sets on weekends to watch sporting competitions. Encouraging workers to compete against each other to see who can make the most sales or get the best customer-service reports is a typical motivational device in our culture. Surely it is safe to say that competition exerts some motivating power, but how might it relate to individuals' more subtle desires to motivate themselves and to feel a sense of personal autonomy?

One student in the seminar suggested that competition could focus people on winning rather than on the activity itself, much like rewards draw people's attention away from the activity itself. Furthermore, it could be that competition creates a pressure pushing people toward particular ends and away from the activity itself. If this were so, it too could undermine intrinsic motivation. Some athletes in the room thought the idea preposterous. It stimulates intrinsic motivation, they said. So we decided to take the question into the lab.

We modified the Soma paradigm to fit the question we were asking. Subjects worked on three puzzles in the presence of an experimental accomplice who posed as a second subject. Half the subjects were told that their task was to win the competition—to beat their opponent by solving the puzzles more quickly. The other half were simply asked to work as quickly as they could; there was no mention of competing or winning.

The accomplice always let the actual subjects finish first, which in the competition condition meant that the subjects won all three of their competitions. Results of the study indicated that those subjects who had competed displayed less subsequent intrinsic motivation than those who had simply been asked to do their best. The experience of competing had undermined their intrinsic motivation for the interesting task. Apparently, they felt pressured and controlled by the competition (even though they won it), and that seemed to decrease their desire to solve these puzzles just for the fun of it.

While interesting, this whole set of findings is quite unsettling, because all the events that were found to undermine intrinsic motivation are events that most people encounter regularly in their ongoing daily lives. These forces—the alarm clock that wakes them up, the pressures to get the kids to school on time and themselves to work on time, and the rewards, deadlines, threats, and evaluations they cope with while at work—are all aspects of people's lives that can apparently leave them feeling pushed around, that can leave them feeling like pawns.

At this point, an obvious question arises. Do all these research results imply that, in order not to weaken intrinsic motivation, people should be allowed to do anything they please? Fortunately, it does not. But before we can tackle the difficult questions of how to provide structures and set limits on behavior without killing a person's spirit, we need to address the inverse of what we have just been reporting. We need to consider what factors might increase intrinsic motivation.

It seemed that if controlling people—that is, pressuring them to behave in particular ways—diminishes their feelings of self-determination, then giving them choices about how to behave ought to enhance them. Some colleagues and I tested this hunch. We used a variant of the puzzle-solving paradigm yet again. Subjects in one group were offered a choice about which puzzles to work on and how long to spend on each. Subjects in the other group were assigned the puzzles and time limits selected by corresponding subjects in the first group.

As expected, given that a comprehensive picture was beginning to emerge from all these experiments, the subjects who had been offered the simple choices spent more time playing with the puzzles and reported liking them more than the subjects not offered choice. The opportunity to make even these small choices had made a difference in their experience and had strengthened their intrinsic motivation.

Once again, it was the issue of autonomy versus control, with its various shadings, that was at the heart of the matter. People who were asked to do a particular task but allowed the freedom of having

some say in how to do it were more fully engaged by the activity—
they enjoyed it more—than people who were not treated as unique
individuals.

It is forever being said that people need to be controlled more,
that they need to be told what to do and held accountable for doing
it. But nothing in these experiments has given credence to that view
as the typical condition of life. Of course, limit setting is important,
as we will see, but an overemphasis on control and discipline seems
to be off the mark. It represents a demeaning depiction of human
experience, and its primary function may just be to provide certain
people with an easy rationalization for exerting power over others.

Providing choice, in the broad sense of that term, is a central
feature in supporting a person's autonomy. It is thus important that
people in positions of authority begin to consider how to provide
more choice. Even in crowded classrooms, fast-paced offices, or har-
ried doctors' offices there are ways, and the more creative one is, the
more possibilities one will find. Why not give students choice about
what field trips to take and what topics to write their papers about,
for example? Why not let the work group participate in the decision
of how to allocate responsibilities? And why not let patients take
part in planning their treatment regimen? It is not always easy to
provide choice, but it has become increasingly clear that there will be
positive advantages if you do.

The main thing about meaningful choice is that it engenders willingness. It encourages people to fully endorse what they are doing; it
pulls them into the activity and allows them to feel a greater sense of
volition; it decreases their alienation. When you provide people
choice, it leaves them feeling as if you are responsive to them as individuals. And providing choice may very well lead to better, or
more workable, solutions than the ones you would have imposed.

Someone told me a story about his aunt who had been taking
hypertension medication for years—or rather, she was supposed
to have been taking it for years. But she was never very good about

following the prescription, and she frequently ended up in the emergency room with fainting spells, ministrokes, and chest pains. Her doctor gave her a pretty hard time about it. He had prescribed the medication, told her that she had to take it every morning, and emphasized the awful things that could happen to her if she did not take it as prescribed. Well, she did not take it as prescribed, and of course some of those awful things (though, fortunately, not the worst of them) did happen to her. In one conversation a few years ago, the nephew asked her why she didn't take her medication each morning. She said she just never seemed to remember it.

He saw her again not long ago, and she told him she was doing much better. She was taking her medication faithfully, and she hadn't been to the emergency room in months. What had changed? Well, for one thing, she had changed doctors. And she said she liked this new doctor better. The interesting thing is that the new doctor had had a long talk with her about the medication, and during the talk he had asked her what time of day she thought would be the best time for her to take it. (Medically, it did not really matter.) She thought about it for a minute, and then she said, "The evening, just before I go to bed." If she took it then, she said, she could build it into her routine. She always has a glass of milk before she goes to bed, she said, and she could take her medication with her glass of milk. It all made such good sense. Her doctor had given her a choice about how to handle her own medication, and it had made a big difference. Now she takes it every day, and the illness intrudes less into her life.

When the doctor gave this woman choice, two things seem to have happened that led her to follow through more responsibly. First, she could organize the task with respect to her own idiosyncrasies (the routine of her nightly glass of milk). In other words, the chosen schedule was a more workable one for her. And second, the woman felt responded to—empowered, really—by the opportunity to choose. Her inherent motivation had been enhanced because the choice supported her autonomy. Of course there are times when doctors should make the decisions, because they alone have certain expertise, but if they provide choice whenever it is possible, positive motivational effects are likely to result.

When choice is offered, of course, it is essential that the person being offered choice have the information necessary for making a meaningful decision. An accountant who asks how you would like to handle a potential deduction without laying out the full array of information you need to make a thoughtful decision is not providing you a meaningful choice. "Is it really legal, or would it be pushing the limits of the law?" "What are the implications for other sections of the tax return?" And so on. To experience a sense of choice, you need to know (or be able to find out) the possibilities, the constraints, the hidden features. Without such information, being given a choice will feel more like a burden than a support for autonomy. It may well engender anxiety, and without adequate information, people are more likely to make mistakes.

In 1977, Richard Ryan moved to the University of Rochester. His strong background in philosophy and psychoanalytic psychology complemented my training in mathematics and experimental psychology. We quickly discovered that, although we were coming at problems from different directions, we shared a fundamental interest in psychological questions about human freedom and self-regulation, questions about authenticity, responsibility, and alienation. We soon began collaborating on research.

In one early discussion, Ryan focused on the point that the impact of a reward should depend on how the person interprets it—on its psychological meaning for that person. It was clear from the earlier studies that people frequently interpret rewards as controls, as means of pressuring them to behave in particular ways. But it would seem that under the right circumstances people might experience rewards simply as an acknowledgment by another that they have done well at something. If that were true, Ryan suggested, it ought to be possible to give rewards in a way that does not undermine intrinsic motivation.

One thing that Ryan thought might make a difference is the intention and style of the person who is administering the reward. Rewards are often used by people to impose their power on others. They give the rewards with the intention to control—or, more euphemistically, "to motivate"—so the rewards are likely to be experienced by their recipient as controlling.

To take one unhappy example, think about the college student who had grown up in a wealthy family in suburban New York. Both his parents were attorneys and they wanted him to become a lawyer, as well. He began taking prelaw courses, as expected, but soon discovered that his real love was film. In a conversation with his parents over a vacation break, he made clear his desire to change majors. The response was a decided lack of enthusiasm. "Fine," they said, "but you're on your own. We will no longer pay your tuition if that's how you are going to waste your college years."

Although these parents had been giving their son a remarkable (and expensive) opportunity to study at an excellent university, it was also true that implicit in their giving was a control. These parents saw money not as a family resource to be shared, but rather as something that could be used to shape their son as they desired. And it is likely that their intentions were somehow being communicated, even if only subtly. The showdown over tuition badly strained the relationship between parents and son, and for his own sake, the son emotionally distanced himself from his parents.

Despite such examples, Ryan suggested that if instead of having the intention to control, the person administering rewards intends them simply as an acknowledgment—as an indicator of accomplishment, so to speak—it is possible that the recipient will not experience them as controlling. In that case, the rewards should not undermine intrinsic motivation.

People's real intentions, when giving rewards, are likely to be communicated by the style and locution they exhibit when dispensing the rewards. Thus, Ryan decided to do a study in which rewards would be administered with two different interpersonal styles. One would be controlling, conveyed with words like "should" and "have to," while the other would be noncontrolling—more egalitarian, if you will.

Ryan trained experimenters in how to execute the two different interpersonal climates that children might encounter in homes, or workers in offices, and it turned out that Ryan had been right. Approach did count. When rewards were given with a controlling style, they had a substantially negative effect on intrinsic motivation, and they left people feeling more pressured and less interested. But when they were given in a noncontrolling way, simply as an acknowledgment of good work, they did not have the detrimental effects. These results therefore seemed to be saying that it is the controlling intent of rewards that sabotages their attempts to motivate others, destroying the very motivation they had been intended to promote.

Pragmatically, this finding confirmed that it is possible to administer rewards in ways that minimize their negative effects. When people proffer rewards without intending to control there is less likelihood that the rewards will have deleterious effects. This is a quite tricky issue, however, because one has to couple this finding with the fact that in the previous reward studies, a very neutral stance had been adopted by the experimenters and, nevertheless, the rewards were undermining. What that means is that the cards are clearly stacked in one direction, that rewards do tend to carry a controlling significance for people. Yes, rewards can be used in a way that is not detrimental to intrinsic motivation—to a person's innate vitality—but the people administering those rewards have to be very conscientious in how they use rewards in order to counteract the most likely effect, which is negative.

I have a friend, a six-year-old girl named Lisa, who has been taking violin lessons for nearly a year. It is the only instrument taught in her small urban school, and many of her friends also take lessons. Lisa is a perfectionist, and in spite of having very accepting parents, she is extremely hard on herself if she fails at something.

When she first started lessons, she was often tense about practicing, feeling that whatever playing she did was not good enough. She became resistant to practicing in order to avoid the inner conflict it engendered. At one point, a few months into her lessons, the teacher introduced a new system to motivate the students to practice more. They would get a star for practicing a specified amount of time each week, and when enough stars had accumulated they would receive a "treasure." Interestingly, Lisa seemed to become less resistant to practice sessions. She still seemed tense about the actual practicing, but she was less evasive of the sessions themselves.

This turn of events intrigued me. The structure of specifying the amount of time she should practice, along with the promise of a reward for adhering, had seemed to make it easier for Lisa. When she had done the specified amount, she could stop and feel she had done enough. But something else began to happen during practice sessions; Lisa would watch the clock. She was no more interested in the violin itself, but she was a lot more interested in completing the practice sessions.

One Sunday a couple of months later, Lisa repeatedly mentioned to her parents that she had to practice, but she also seemed less willing than she had been recently. At one point, her mother said, "Okay, let's go practice now." As was often the case, her mother sat with her while she practiced, but things did not go well. Lisa fooled around rather than practice seriously. She assumed sloppy positions, and she wanted only to play well-learned, easy pieces. Her mother, nonetheless, encouraged her to persist. So Lisa would try something new, make a mistake, and then start to cry. The tension became palpable.

A little later, Lisa's father went into the room to relieve his wife. He said to Lisa, "Let's put the violin away for now. You can practice tomorrow night and I'll sit with you then." Agitated, Lisa said, "No, I *have* to do it now!" So she picked up her violin and started. Almost immediately she made a mistake and got upset. Her father took the violin, and put it on a shelf across the room. He let her be upset for a couple of minutes, and then he began to quietly talk with her about it. He was interested in why she was putting so much pressure on herself.

"Why do you have to practice today?" he asked her. Well, it

took some reassuring and talking before he finally got to the issue. Lisa finally revealed that if she didn't practice she wouldn't get her star, and if she didn't get this star, her friends would get their treasure, but she wouldn't get hers. The intensity of the pressure this six-year-old had put on herself because of her teacher's use of an "incentive" was nothing short of astounding.

Lisa's father asked her what the treasure would be. She didn't know, but he told her that whatever it was, if she did not get it from her violin teacher, he would get one for her. Lisa was amazed, and she said, "You mean I don't have to practice to get the treasure?" "No," he said, "you can have it whether you practice or not." Much of the tension lifted, and her practicing went more easily after that. Playing the violin can, after all, be fun.

Advocates of using rewards to motivate children often tell stories like the first half of this one—stories about how the offer of a reward helps get children to practice their violins, do their chores, keep up with their homework, or whatever. I'm always a little skeptical even though I know that rewards are not all bad. I'm skeptical because it is clear that rewards often have negative, though unintended, consequences that the advocates are usually not willing to acknowledge. Rewards might ensure certain behaviors—like more regular practice sessions—but the behaviors they ensure may not really be what we are after. The example with Lisa made that point very clearly.

The introduction of the reward structure helped her at first because it gave her information about what would be a good amount of time for practice. But some discussion and structure, without the use of rewards, might have served just as well. In other words, a negotiation about the amount of time could have accomplished the end of overcoming her initial resistance—and that would not have had the same negative effects.

Offering rewards in a *noncontrolling* way requires a kind of deep honesty that often eludes people. People say they are *not* trying to mold their children, for instance, that they are simply expressing appreciation, leading by example, or providing the children with just the sort of thing the children really want or need. But thoughtful reflection often reveals that in fact the adults really are using the rewards to pressure the children, even though what they are pressuring the children to do might be in the children's best interests. The real question that all this poses is whether pressuring children with rewards to do something that is good for them is the best way to achieve the desired end.

The issue of pressure and control, of course, goes far beyond the use of rewards. One of the important things about Ryan's study of administering rewards in two different ways—one way that emphasizes pressure and control, and the other that does not—is that it suggests that many other events or occurrences that had been found to undermine intrinsic motivation, might not have to if used more sensitively.

The competition study that my students and I had previously done had become somewhat controversial. People just did not want to believe that competition diminishes intrinsic motivation. After the profound results that emerged from Ryan's reward study, a colleague, Johnmarshall Reeve, and I decided to look into the same issue with respect to competition. In essence, we had one group who won a competition after having been pressured to win—we used the old "Vince Lombardi tactic" of telling them that winning is *everything*—and another group who won a competition without having the added pressure. Interestingly, our results paralleled Ryan's. When we oriented people toward the competition by really emphasizing the importance of beating the other, the competition was quite detrimental to their intrinsic motivation. However, when we did not add this pressure, but instead simply encouraged them to do their best and try to finish first, the competition was not detrimental.

In this competition study, we also had a nonpressured group that lost the competition, and here we found an extremely low level of intrinsic motivation. All of the findings, when taken together, indicate that competition does not necessarily undermine intrinsic motivation, but it is a quite delicate matter. Pressuring people to win, which seems to come so naturally in competitive situations, is likely to have a negative effect, even for winners. And, of course, for losers, the effect is worse.

B y taking a general stance against reliance on rewards, demands, threats, surveillance, competition, and critical evaluations as avenues for *motivating* people's behavior, I am not by any means advocating permissiveness. The use of goals, structures, and limit setting is often important in schools, organizations, and cultures, even if people cannot be expected to like them. It's just not reasonable, for example, to allow children to hurl paint at each other (the noble savage, aside) or to allow workers to stroll into work whenever they feel like it. The really important question, then, is how can we avoid being permissive, without creating gridlock? How can autonomy support and limit setting coexist? How can standards and limits be used so the person in the one-down position can live within the limits and still retain a feeling of self-initiation, and thus not lose intrinsic motivation?

Autonomy support, which is the opposite of control, means being able to take the other person's perspective and work from there. It means actively encouraging self-initiation, experimentation, and responsibility, and it may very well require setting limits. But autonomy support functions through encouragement, not pressure. Providing that encouragement without slipping over into control would seem to be possible, but by no means easy. We already knew that being autonomy supportive can be more difficult—requiring more effort and more skill—than being coercive.

Given what he had learned from the study of different styles of rewarding, Ryan decided to explore the question of whether limits and autonomy could coexist. He worked with Richard Koestner (now a professor at McGill University in Montreal) and identified a classic situation requiring both limits and creative autonomy: children's art. The idea was to engage kids (five- and six-year-olds) in a creative, but potentially messy, task of painting a picture. Limits concerning neatness were set in two different ways—the conventional, controlling way, and a noncontrolling, autonomy-supportive way. The controlling way was simple: use pressuring language ("be a good boy/girl and keep the materials neat" or "do as you should and don't mix up the colors").

The autonomy-supportive way, which involves minimizing pressure by avoiding controlling language and allowing as much choice as possible, required more subtlety. In setting limits, there is always a potential conflict because you are asking people to do something they might not want to do. That's the whole point of the limits. Koestner and Ryan thought that acknowledging this conflict might help because it conveys an appreciation of the children's perspective and thus should lessen the extent to which they would feel externally controlled. In the autonomy-supportive limits group, they said, "I know that sometimes it's really fun to just slop the paint around, but here the materials and room need to be kept nice for the other children who will use them."

Encouragingly, from the point of view of our accumulating body of work, the results were dramatic. Even these simple variations in instructions made a difference. The autonomy-supportive condition seemed to have a liberating effect on the children, while the controlling condition had a debilitating effect. The children who sensed that the adults at least understood them were more intrinsically motivated and more enthusiastic than the children for whom the limits had been controlling. It was as if one could see right here both the power and the perils of setting rules in all sorts of life situations where someone in a one-up position can maximize people's experience or dampen it—depending on interpersonal style.

Limit setting is extremely important for promoting responsibility, and the findings of this study are critical for how to do it. By setting limits in an autonomy-supportive way—in other words, by aligning yourself with the person being limited, recognizing that he or she is a proactive subject, rather than an object to be manipulated or controlled—it is possible to encourage responsibility without undermining authenticity.

FOUR

Intrinsic and Extrinsic Motivation

The Yields of Each

A friend had a disturbing experience recently. With his son on the brink of college—which, for many parents, requires such a monumental financial sacrifice that they are stunned when the reality of it hits them—he called in an adviser he had been told was in the business of assisting parents in finding college financial aid. The pleasant, enthusiastic adviser showed up and, with an apparent sense of warmth and caring, began inquiring about their family aspirations and their available finances. Hearing the responses, he said he was just the fellow to save them real money by helping them fill out all the financial forms. That way, he could get them what he called their "fair share."

It happens that this family is modestly affluent, with too much money in mutual funds to make them eligible for many kinds of aid, so the adviser suggested that they place it in the name of the husband's mother. As luck would have it, because the amiable fellow also worked for an insurance company, he could offer them the opportunity to open an annuity account for the husband's mother and quickly move the funds there. Then he could fill out the forms reflecting the family's newfound poverty. And now that he knew so much about them, he couldn't resist saying, "You know you are grossly underinsured," and he was in a position to provide them with the "appropriate amount of life insurance."

The couple felt very uneasy about the transfer of money to the mother. It just didn't seem right. But with their thinking blurred by all the fast talk, they wrote a check for his fee of $200. Later, when the fog lifted, they regretted it. He wasn't really a college-aid counselor at all. Or, if he was, that was only a sideline. He was in fact an insurance salesman working for commissions, and he saw in them an easy mark—perfect customers. All he had to do was set the hook, persuade them to put themselves in his hands as he contrived to deceive the governmental and university scholarship apparatus, and he would make long-term buyers out of them. Ultimately, the couple refused to go along, and they chalked up the $200 loss to a mistake in judgment.

When I heard the story, it struck me that it illustrates something fundamental about the use of money (in this case, sales commissions) as a means of motivating sales. It makes the sale become everything, so the temptation is there to deceive and manipulate if that's what's needed to make the sale. Extrinsic control all too often gets people focused only on the outcomes, and that leads to shortcuts that may be unsavory, or just sad. As such, they are a far cry from the uplifting experiences that intrinsic motivation can bring.

There is an aspect of intrinsic motivation that sets it quite apart from extrinsic control. It has been implicit in the discussions thus far, but I want to emphasize it for a moment. It is an aspect that is almost spiritual. It has to do with life itself: It is vitality, dedication, transcendence. It is what one experiences at those times that Robert Henri called "more than ordinary moments of existence."

There is a long history of work in literature and Eastern philosophy, among other disciplines, emphasizing that such experiences— call them heightened awareness, even satori—are of value in their own right. University of Chicago psychologist Mihaly Csikszent-mihalyi refers to these experiences as being in a state of "flow," when time seems to collapse and disappear, when intensity in the process takes over and the thrill is so great that one hates seeing it end and can't wait to get back to it. Tennis players might feel it, and so might surgeons, writers, painters, and dancers. Intense experiences like these ennoble life, make it vastly more enjoyable and ultimately result in greater self-understanding and self-honesty. They give us the opportunity to observe what real, deep interest feels like—the joy of it—as opposed to the drudgery that external control tends to bring.

I have always believed that the *experience* of intrinsic motivation is its own justification. Smelling the roses, being enthralled by how the pieces of a puzzle fit together, seeing the sunlight as it dances in the clouds, feeling the thrill of reaching a mountain summit: These are experiences that need yield nothing more to be fully justified. And one might go so far as to argue that a life devoid of such experiences is hardly a life at all.

But modern society is not very concerned about all that. Modern society has what philosopher Charles Taylor recently referred to as the malaise of "instrumental reason." Everything gets evaluated in terms of its bottom-line yield—the cost-benefit ratio, so to speak. Sadly, even things that should be evaluated by other criteria, like personal relationships, seem to have come under the dark eye of instrumental reason.

"To feel alive, to be interested and engrossed in an activity, to be in a state of flow, is all well and good," some will say, "but what does it get you?" These people want results. They want "noteworthy pictures," and they don't care whether the painter is in "a high state of functioning" while creating them. They want high test scores, and they are not terribly concerned if the students feel good or are interested in school. They want profits, and they do not pay much attention to the professional or personal development of the employees.

Of course it is important to attend to the outcomes of motivation, and although intrinsic motivation is a desirable end in its own right, Ryan and I have devoted considerable attention to exploring the concrete consequences of being intrinsically motivated versus externally controlled. Without verifying that it has concrete advantages, we would be on shaky grounds advocating its promotion in schools, homes, and offices—indeed, in society more generally. So we set out to clarify whether people, when they are intrinsically motivated, also achieve at high levels. Robert Henri hinted at the answer with his powerful intuitive observation that intrinsic motivation is in "back of every true work of art." But what does the research say?

The arena of education seemed like ripe territory for beginning this research because countless people had suggested that motivation is the key to success in education. Certainly, learning seems to be great fun for some people and quite tedious for others, and it was the whole issue of motivation for learning that got me interested in intrinsic motivation in the first place. Fortunately, the outcomes of education—learning, performance, and adjustment—can be reliably measured, which is essential for doing research.

In education, grades (sometimes accompanied by other things like gold stars or dean's lists) are the primary means of extrinsic control. They are considered incentives, and it is assumed that people will be motivated to learn so they can get good grades. In one learning experiment I did with former student Carl Benware, we considered the issue of grades as a motivator. We had two groups of college students spend about three hours learning some complex material on neurophysiology—on the machinery of the brain. Half of these students were told they would be tested and graded on their learning, and the others were told they would have the opportunity to put the material to active use by teaching it to others. We expected that learning in order to be tested would feel very controlling to the students, whereas learning to put the information to active use would feel like an exciting challenge. After students had learned the material, we assessed their intrinsic motivation with a questionnaire, and we found, as expected, that those who learned in order to be tested were less intrinsically motivated.

Then we took it one step further to get at the main issue—the actual learning that had gone on. We tested both groups, even though the one group had not expected it, and the results showed that the students who learned in order to put the material to active use displayed considerably greater conceptual understanding of the material than did the students who learned in order to be tested. As the research made clear, yet again, well-intentioned people—for instance, people employing tests to motivate learning—are unwittingly defeating the desire to learn in those people they are attempting to help.

Ryan, working with Wendy Grolnick (now a faculty member at Clark University), did another learning study, this time with elementary-school children. Two groups of children were asked to read two short passages from grade-level textbooks. Some of the children were told that they would be tested and graded on what they read; others were just asked to read the material without any mention of a test. Those who learned the material without expecting to be tested displayed superior conceptual understanding relative to those who were expecting to be tested.

An additional, interesting piece of information was picked up in this study. The children who expected to be tested displayed greater rote memorization than those not expecting the test. It seems that when people learn with the expectation of being evaluated, they focus on memorizing facts, but they don't process the information as fully, so they don't grasp the concepts as well. On the face of it, this suggests that the type of learning context that should be created, depends on which type of learning one hopes to foster—rote memorization or conceptual understanding. But there's a catch here—and a quite fascinating one—that was discovered in a final phase of this study.

Another adult visited the classrooms of these elementary-school children a week after they had participated in the experiment. The adult introduced himself and reminded the children of their experience the week before with the woman who had given them the material to read. He then said he would like to ask them some questions about what they had read. On that test, all the children recalled less than they had the week before when they had just read the material, but that's to be expected. Stunningly, however, those who had learned expecting to be tested had forgotten much more. Their superior rote memorization was no longer in evidence a few days later. Evidently, they memorized the material for the test, and when the test was over, they pulled the plug and let it drain out. Using computer jargon, Grolnick and Ryan referred to this as a "core dump."

With both college students and elementary-school children, the research indicates quite convincingly that the strategy of giving tests is not necessarily productive if the objective is long-term learning. Recently, results comparable to these have been found in other cultures as well, even among the Japanese who, Americans suppose, have become such fierce economic adversaries in part because of the pressure exerted on them in schools.

Masaharu Kage, a young Japanese educational psychologist, performed experiments in his native public schools aimed at assessing the validity of our results in his culture, and he found surprisingly strong support for our position. In one of the studies, he gave quizzes to students in several classrooms, but he did it in two different ways. In some classes, the quizzes were evaluated by the teacher and used as part of the grade for the course, while in other classes, the students went over their own quizzes to monitor their own performance, but the quizzes were not used as part of the course grading system. Kage found that the use of evaluative quizzes to motivate learning led to lowered intrinsic motivation and to poorer performance on the final examination than did the self-monitored, nonevaluative quizzes. In Japanese society, it seems, there are the same learning advantages to minimizing rather than maximizing the pressures. The finding may very well characterize people in general, not just people in America.

So, it seems pretty clear that learning will be greater when prompted by intrinsic motivation rather than external controls. What about other qualities of human behavior? Recall the limit-setting study reported at the end of the last chapter, in which young children painted pictures under conditions of controlling limits versus autonomy-supportive limits. Those who painted with the controlling limits were less intrinsically motivated than those who painted with the autonomy-supportive limits. Well, there was a twist to that study as well.

The researchers also looked at the quality of the actual pictures that the children painted, using a method developed by psychologist

Teresa Amabile. They took all the paintings made by the children in the two groups and mixed them together. Then they gave all the pictures to half a dozen judges who rated both the creativity and the technical merits of each picture. The quality score was a combination of these two factors. After the ratings were finished, the researchers separated the paintings back into the original two groups and they calculated the average quality ratings of the pictures in each group. They found that the children who had painted with the autonomy-supportive limits and had been more intrinsically motivated, also painted better quality pictures—they used more colors, more original designs, and more varied motifs—than did the children with the controlling limits. Robert Henri was right again: People who are more intrinsically motivated to paint not only have a heightened experience, but they are also more likely to produce a real work of art.

Other studies have revealed that people perform less well at problem solving when they are working for an extrinsic reward than when they are intrinsically motivated. In fact, several studies have confirmed that the performance of any activity requiring resourcefulness, deep concentration, intuition, or creativity is likely to be impaired when controls are used as a motivational strategy. And, of course, it is also the case that people will enjoy it less—feel less good about the experience—when external controls are the reason for their behavior.

There are some tasks, the simple routine ones, where rewards and controls may serve to speed up performance, particularly if the rewards are based on how many units of work are done. But it is important to keep in mind that improving performance in these ways may have other, negative effects for the individuals performing the task, and those effects may come out in other ways, like developing a tendency to do only what they are paid to do, and possibly even engaging in subtle sabotage. Whatever the case, you can be sure that these rewards won't be engendering a deep commitment to the work and the organization.

So where does this leave us? What has been discovered in the research on the qualities of intrinsically motivated (versus externally controlled) behavior? Intrinsic motivation is associated with richer experience, better conceptual understanding, greater creativity, and improved problem solving, relative to external controls. Not only do controls undermine intrinsic motivation and engagement with activities but—and here is a bit of bad news for people focused on the bottom line—they have clearly detrimental effects on performance of any tasks that require creativity, conceptual understanding, or flexible problem solving.

A s we reflect on how the use of excessive control—especially through the use of extrinsic rewards—can undermine intrinsic motivation and the quality of performance, it is important to keep in mind that rewards and other controls do have motivating power. People's behavior can, at least to some extent, be controlled in the sense that people will do what they have to in order to get extrinsic rewards, avoid punishments, or win competitions. (Remember those seals in the Prospect Park Zoo.) Still, there are pragmatic problems with relying on rewards and controls to motivate people that are important to keep in mind when you decide to use that motivational strategy.

The first is that once you have begun to use rewards to control people, you cannot easily go back. As the experiments have shown, when behaviors become instrumental to monetary rewards—in other words, when people behave to get rewards—those behaviors will last only so long as the rewards are forthcoming. In some cases that may be fine, but in most cases the activities we reward are ones that we would like to have persist long after the rewards have stopped. If you ran a fitness center, for example, and you used a reward system to encourage people to exercise, you would want those people to remain active after the rewards stopped. But it is pretty likely that if they exercise for the rewards, they will stop exercising when there are no longer rewards. And if you offered rewards to your children for learning—a dollar for each A on their report cards, let's say—you would want the children to remain enthusiastic about learning after your reward system was terminated. But it is not at all clear that they would. Again, remember how those seals stopped their delightful displays when the bag of fish disappeared.

The second problem, which was already alluded to, is that once people are oriented toward rewards, they will all too likely take the shortest or quickest path to get them. Usually, however, the shortest path is not what we hope to promote. Remember how Lisa watched the clock and wanted to play the easiest songs. Even more troubling, remember how the insurance salesman deceived and manipulated to try to make his sale.

I also know this to be true from one of my own early experiences. When I was in first grade, during the first week of school, our teacher, Miss Cook, told us about all the books in a bookcase at the back of the room. Like most five-year-olds, I was bursting to become a good reader, and Miss Cook warmly encouraged us to read the books. She explained the sign-out procedure, for it was to be like a library, with each book accounted for. Then, just to inject a bit of added incentive, she told us that the student who read the most books would receive a prize at the end of the year. Miss Cook didn't say what the prize would be, and the end of the year must have seemed a long way off. But I knew I wanted the prize whatever it might be. And more to the point, I suppose, I wanted the approval that would likely accompany the prize.

Somehow I managed to figure out that the prize would really be awarded to the person who *signed out* the most books rather than the person who *read* the most books. So I started signing out books, one after another. I don't recall how many I read, but it was certainly fewer than the number I signed out. When the end of the year finally came, I had won the big box of Crayola crayons. It's sad to look back on it now. The crayons were nice, at the time, but they're long gone. Gone, too, is the reading that might have happened, the discovery that could have been mine. And how I got away with it, I will never know.

I'm embarrassed as I tell the story now, feeling a bit like the insurance salesman. It is as if I had sold a piece of my morality for a box of crayons. But, of course, five-year-olds don't understand much about morality because moral reasoning develops in systematic ways at predictable times in a child's life, and it is still quite primitive for children at that age.

In the last few years, many teachers have told me stories that remind me of my experience with Miss Cook. For example, there is the case of a perhaps well-intentioned program offered by a pizza franchise, in which students accumulated points for reading books which they turned in for free pizzas. The implicit message, of course, is that pizzas are more interesting than books, and a number of teachers have remarked that programs such as this make it harder, rather than easier, to stimulate students' interest in reading. No doubt, these students want the pizzas, and they'll do what they have to do to get them. They'll just say they read the books if they can get away with it, or they'll just read the books superficially. What's more, even if the pizzas do prompt some reading, it is very unlikely that the students will be interested in continuing to read after the free pizzas are no longer available.

The problem is in the use of reward structures to motivate something that could be made exciting in its own right. In retrospect, it is easy to see that Miss Cook should have focused on the joys of reading in some informative, engaging way. But she was caught up in a widely held, profoundly erroneous theory of human motivation. She thought she was doing the right thing, but she lacked some of the wisdom of the Jewish tailor on Main Street.

This same type of problem occurs in the workplace all the time, and we see it most keenly with respect to quality control. Pay people in accord with how much they produce, and they will produce a lot, but the quality is not likely to be up to snuff. The typical response is to become even more controlling, to set up elaborate policing systems of one sort or another. But really that is just escalating the battle rather than solving the problem. People can be pretty creative in getting around rules, they can be pretty clever in finding the shortest path to a reward. The junk-bond kings and arbitrageurs of the 1980s could not have made this point any more convincingly.

The junk-bond kings were, of course, extreme examples. A more common instance is contained in a story recently told by a friend. It occurred in a publishing house, but it could have been any business. Profit and loss statements were a big deal in that company, of course. Actually, a bit too big of a deal. It seems that bonuses, which people had become dependent on both for the money itself and for the ego boost it provided, were awarded to each manager on the basis of the P & L statement for the group he or she managed.

What often happened, and not surprisingly, is that toward the end of the year, editors would rush books into print that would better have waited until the following year. They needed the numbers, so they directed their creativity and resourcefulness toward getting those numbers, rather than toward effective performance. Obviously, doing that is a bad business decision, but the proffered bonus seemed to promote a lot of that.

P ay-for-performance is a revered concept in management circles. It's classic carrot and stick. "Piece-rate payment," which was the central motivational technique in the Scientific Management approach developed early in this century by Frederick Winslow Taylor, is the quintessential pay-for-performance method. It involves compensating employees for each specific piece of work they do. Count the bars of pig iron a man moves in eight hours and pay him so much per bar. That's his wage for today. The reasoning, of course, is that if he wants more money, he will move more bars tomorrow.

Sales commissions also represent an example of the pure pay-for-performance concept. As with the burly, immigrant worker moving pig iron for piece-rate payments early in the century, the well-groomed, verbally fluent sales rep of today can determine his own pay. Sell more software packages or minivans and make more money. Sell more insurance policies, even if you have to lie a little to do it, and you will become more affluent.

At the top of the corporate world, pay-for-performance takes forms such as profit-sharing stock options. The rationale behind all these motivational incentives is that "money talks." People want money, so if you structure the situation correctly you can get them to do what you want.

The results of the studies cast further doubt on the efficacy of these pay-for-performance practices, however. Of course, these practices can motivate people, but in the process, they will likely encourage shortcuts and undermine intrinsic motivation. They will draw people's attention away from the job itself, toward the rewards it can yield, and that without doubt will result in less effective, less creative problem solving. In a time of major problems facing the business world, in a time when thoughtful, visionary problem solving is what's needed, too many companies have taken the easy road by falling into a pattern of relying on glamorous incentives rather than promoting involvement with the job and commitment to the company.

Money is the medium of exchange in all modern economic systems, so monetary payments rewards have to be dispensed. But there are better and worse ways of doing that. It is better, for example, not to think about rewards as a way to motivate people. Rewards are part of the work contract, so you would not have workers without rewards. But research suggests that, to the extent that rewards are "used" for any function other than retaining workers, it ought be merely to acknowledge or signify a job well done. Rewards can be used as a way to express appreciation, but the more they are used as motivators—like the bonus plan in the publishing house—the more likely it is that they will have negative effects.

Treats and gifts are nice for children, and grandparents love being able to give them. But again, the less they are given contingently, for being a good boy or a good girl, and the less they are used to motivate children (to do well in school, say), the more positive (or less negative) will be their effects.

Another important point about administering rewards is that they need, in some important sense, to be equitable. In other words, people need to feel that their rewards are commensurate with their contributions, and are equitable relative to what other people around them are earning. Equitable rewards mean that people who give more to an organization will get more from it. But that is a tricky matter because the idea tempts people to use rewards to try to motivate people to give more, which, of course, highlights the controlling aspect of the rewards. Instead, by de-emphasizing rewards as a motivational strategy and playing them down as an aspect of the work setting, they can be administered equitably simply as a fact of the implicit contract of work. That way, they will be less likely to initiate the processes that have been shown to have detrimental effects.

FIVE

Engaging the World with a Sense of Competence

S everal times prior to the demise of the Soviet Empire in 1989, I served as a consultant for the Council of Ministers in the poor and weary nation of Bulgaria. The lack of motivation among the citizenry was extraordinary. The society as a whole seemed depressed. People did what they had to do in order not to get into trouble, of course, but most of them had little constructive involvement in the productive activities of the nation's enterprises. Whereas in the United States, instrumentalities (or linkages) between people's behavior and their desired outcomes are built into the system and widely used to motivate achievement, in Bulgaria they were remarkably absent. Simply stated, there was nothing riding on whether or not people were productive, so there was a bare minimum of active compliance toward productive ends.

I remember one visit to a state-owned manufacturing company. I went with my interpreter, Julian Usunov (who now, under the new system, is a management consultant), and we were shown around by the general manager of the company. It was the middle of the afternoon, and we went into one cavernous room, with a couple of dozen workstations. Each station had a machine for working with metal—lathes, drills, presses, and so on. As we entered, we saw a few clusters of idle people sitting or standing around chatting: A room full of Maytag repairmen. When the workers saw us (saw the big boss, that is) some of them ambled back to their workstations, others didn't even bother.

For these workers, and for others in the Bulgarian system, outcomes such as enjoyment of their work, a satisfactory level of pay, and keeping their jobs were not contingent upon their work behavior, so there were no incentives for working. Certainly they would not have enjoyed their work in that cold, dirty room, running those machines, producing pieces of metal that may have had no purpose anyway (the storeroom was full of such things that were headed nowhere), so there would have been no intrinsic rewards for doing good work. Furthermore, the meager extrinsic rewards they received did not serve as motivators because they were not dependent on the quantity or quality of performance. And there were no threats of punishments for failing to work effectively (although, of course, the very fact of being there was itself punishing). Why weren't they just fired? Because under the communist system the ethic was that *everyone* had the right to a job. Pay was dismal, but it was more or less guaranteed. The joke so often told by Bulgarians says it all: "They pretended to pay us and we pretended to work."

A few years ago, Ryan made a trip to China. While there, he was shown through a plant by one of the managers, and he saw behaviors similar to what I had seen in Bulgaria. At one point, he watched a group of about eight people working in a kind of supply depot, where parts were being organized, stored, and distributed. He watched the operation for a few minutes and said to his guide, "It seems to me that they could accomplish the same results with three people. They just seem to get in each other's way." With a tone that bordered on disdain, the manager replied, "Yes, but then what would happen to the others?"

Countries with totalitarian, central-planning systems have been remarkably ineffective in motivating their workers—in getting them to be productive and efficient. Indeed, their approach to motivating work behavior has been far less successful than that built into the American system. The problem is that the central-planning economies lack a fundamental element that is necessary for motivation;

they lack meaningful contingencies—they lack behavior-outcome linkages.

Motivation requires that people see a relationship between their behavior and desired outcome, and instrumentalities are the linkages that allow people to see these behavior-outcome relationships. Instrumentalities can be created at the level of economic systems, at the level of an organization, and at the level of interactions between two individuals such as a parent and child. If people do not believe that their behavior will lead to something they desire—whether the lack of instrumentality is the fault of the system, the organization, or an individual in a one-up position—they will not be motivated. The desired outcomes can be intrinsic satisfactions, or they can be extrinsic rewards, but people have to believe that some outcomes will accrue from their behavior or they will not be motivated to behave. That is what was generally missing in Bulgaria. People did not believe that productive behavior would lead to any meaningful outcomes, so they displayed very little productive behavior.

Built into our system of private ownership and market forces is a set of instrumentalities. Efficiency is paramount, and extrinsic rewards are administered in a way intended to make people efficient. The linkage between behavior and extrinsic rewards is an integral part of the system, and it is lodged in the minds of most individuals within the system. The system has inefficiencies, and people have resorted to manipulating the system as we saw in the last chapter, but still the instrumentalities are there and they have, according to Hong Kong economist Henry Woo, resulted in a remarkably efficient use of human capital when compared to the relative lack of instrumentalities in the central-planning economies of Eastern Europe.

The interesting points in this comparison between Bulgaria and America are: First, that without appropriate instrumentalities, there will not be productive, motivated behavior; but, second, instrumentalities are a double-edged sword—they are the basis for facilitating motivation, but they are also the means through which control can have its profoundly negative effects.

Control, which involves using instrumentalities to pressure people to behave in particular ways, is one form of motivation, and extrinsic-reward contingencies are what allow control to work moderately successfully as a strategy for motivating productivity. The problem, of course, is that control has a variety of substantially negative human consequences.

It is one of the great paradoxes of history that the central-planning economy, which was founded as a tonic for alienation, ended up yielding worse results than the private-ownership system because it used an ineffective approach to control and it typically got coupled with coercive totalitarian regimes. As can be gleaned from our experiments, control itself is alienating, but when it is used ineffectively, as it typically has been by totalitarian regimes, it is utterly disastrous, resulting in widespread lethargy and lack of purpose.

One of the most important points that our experiments have illuminated, and the point that is the basis for hope, is that, although instrumentalities are all too readily used to control, they do not have to be. The most effective parents use reward contingencies in non-controlling ways, rather than controlling ways, and the results are quite positive when they do. The same is true for managers, teachers, and coaches. For example, in the more enlightened U.S. companies, managers understand the importance of intrinsic motivation, so they design more interesting jobs and allow employees the opportunity to participate in decision making—that is, they offer employees choice—so that effective behavior will be instrumental to intrinsic satisfaction. At the same time, they do not rely on extrinsic-reward contingencies to motivate behavior, but instead use rewards simply as a means of acknowledging accomplishment. Extrinsic contingencies do exist in such companies in the sense that people have to perform effectively to keep their jobs and to get promotions, but the contingencies are not emphasized as a means of control.

This point is an extremely important one at the level of policy making as well. When decision makers understand that people can be motivated in either autonomous or controlled ways, and that systems, organizations, and individuals can promote motivation in either autonomy-supportive or controlling ways, they can create policies that are more oriented toward supporting autonomy than toward controlling behavior. Countless decisions get made, in the federal, state, and local governments, as well as in public and private corporations, that profoundly affect people's lives. By thinking about the issues from the perspective of autonomy support rather than control, the decisions will be different, and the effects on people's lives will be different as well.

P eople in the mainstream of American culture know what they need to do to make money, to earn a college degree, to get approval from superiors, to feel a sense of accomplishment, and to have a host of opportunities for themselves and their families. The contingencies are built into our system of life, and these contingencies have worked to motivate a large percentage of the population. But still, in spite of the fact that the American system has served to productively motivate large numbers of people, there are some who have "fallen out of the system," who have not been productively motivated by it, because they have not had access to the contingencies that are central to the system.

Poor schooling provided to some of this country's students, discrimination against some of its citizens, and a defensive indifference that has developed in response to such forces, are among the contributors to the system's having failed to motivate some people—perhaps a quarter of the population—toward productive ends. Thus, although there are instrumentalities within the system, these instrumentalities have failed to work for some people, because those people have not had access to those instrumentalities. For behavior-outcome linkages to serve as motivators, people must understand them, see them as relevant to their lives, and have the capabilities for utilizing them. There are densely populated areas in our inner cities that are full of people who have fallen out of the system because they see no possibility of operating within it. The standard instrumentalities are not relevant to their lives. Poverty, violence, a lack of realistic expectations about a secure future have all left these people feeling more like the Bulgarians during Soviet domination than like the mainstream of American society.

There are many tragic cases; we read about them every day in the paper, and I have heard about them from friends who have worked in inner-city schools. I remember one case quite vividly. He was a smart, often charming young man who had no meaningful family support and no useful role model. When he was in eighth grade, he started dealing drugs, which meant quick money, so he began to wear expensive clothes and jewelry. His teacher saw his potential, and she tried hard to reach him, going the extra mile so to speak, but unfortunately he just drifted further away and eventually stopped showing up in school at all.

From then on, his story got worse. He was involved in various nefarious activities, such as fraudulent telephone sales of fake gems, which landed him in jail for a few months. And he had a string of financial problems, like buying a car and wrecking it before it was paid for. The list of people to whom he owed money and favors was apparently quite long. At one point, when a car hit him on a dark road it nearly severed his right leg. He believed that he had been struck by one of the people he owed money, and perhaps he was. Although his leg was repaired to the point where he could keep it, the limp and pain would always be a problem for him.

The small-time drug dealer had fallen out of the system because he never learned to function within the contingencies of our society—finishing school, committing himself to work, and so on. He tried some easy, seductive contingencies that existed in his circles, but they only landed him in harm's way.

Of course, the lack of motivation brought on by the absence of effective contingencies exists at the interpersonal level, as well as the system's level, and it affects everyone. A recent example I heard about occurred in a middle-class neighborhood. Lisa—the six-year-old violin student—has a neighbor named Jennifer, who is the same age. The girls have been close friends since they were toddlers. Early on a Friday evening not long ago, Jenni's father told her that if she were really good all weekend, he would take her to a toy store on

Monday night and she could have the toy of her choice. Jenni of course was very excited, and all through that evening she was on her very best behavior. She held all her feelings tight within her, so she would look like a good girl to her father. After all, he had emphasized that she had to be *really* good.

On Saturday morning, Lisa went to play with Jenni, as she often did. Within fifteen minutes the two girls had returned to Lisa's house. What had happened was that Jenni's mother had denied her something and she started to cry and shake. Everything she'd been holding in started to come out. Fortunately, her father was off on an errand, so he didn't know what happened. Lisa, being quite astute about such things, invited Jenni to her house where they spent the rest of the day.

What was wrong with this strategy as a means of motivating Jenni to be a good girl? Although the reward was salient enough, the requisite behavior was too vague, so Jenni did not really understand the instrumentality. "Being a good girl" could mean many things, and to Jenni it meant stifling her negative feelings, which led only to trouble. The feelings became too strong to stifle, and although her father did not know about the incident, it resulted in a very unpleasant experience for Jenni and did not lead to the kind of behavior that her father had wanted.

For extrinsic motivation to work as a motivator, there must be clarity about what behaviors are expected, and what outcomes will result from those instrumental behaviors. For Jenni, the outcomes were clear enough but the behaviors were not, so she was not effectively motivated. In most totalitarian systems, and for some people in our system, the same is true; there are not clear linkages between understandable behaviors and desired outcomes, so there is a profound lack of motivation to be a productive member of society.

Although instrumentalities are extremely important for motivation, they alone are not enough to ensure a high level of productive involvement. People must also feel competent at the instrumental behaviors for the instrumentalities to be effective motivators. James Connell and Ellen Skinner, former colleagues in the Human Motivation Program at the University of Rochester, summarized these points by saying that people need to have both the *strategies* and the *capacities* for attaining desired outcomes.

Feeling competent is important both for extrinsic motivation and for intrinsic motivation. Whether behavior is instrumental for extrinsic outcomes such as bonuses and promotions, or for intrinsic outcomes such as enjoyment of the task and feelings of personal accomplishment, people must feel sufficiently competent at the instrumental activities to achieve their desired outcomes. Extrinsic contingencies typically specify competency requirements—in other words, people in one-up positions usually require a certain level of performance quality in order to give the extrinsic outcomes. With intrinsic outcomes, the issue of competency is more integrally intertwined with the enjoyment of the activity itself, and this issue has been the focus of several of our experiments.

The "rewards" linked to intrinsic motivation are the feelings of enjoyment and accomplishment that accrue spontaneously as a person engages freely in the target activities. Thus, feeling competent at the task is an important aspect of one's intrinsic satisfaction. The feeling of being effective is satisfying in its own right, and can even represent the primary draw for a lifelong career. People realize that the more they invest in a job, the better they will get at it, and thus the more intrinsic satisfaction they will experience.

There is a virtually legendary rewrite man on a major daily newspaper (the title "rewrite man," originally bestowed in the days of sexist language, designates a man or woman who remains in the newspaper's office to write news stories from information provided by reporters out in the field and by a variety of other sources). This fellow was so good at what he did and derived such satisfaction from it that he simply had no interest in any other job. He did not mind the late hours. He seemed to revel in the strange rhythm of his job, playing chess with cohorts one minute and then rushing to his computer to tap out a story when the information about some horrifying fire or earthquake came tumbling in. No one doubted that any story he was assigned would turn out pristine in its lucidity. He was simply very good at his work, and the job provided him an enormous amount of intrinsic satisfaction.

Naturally, the company regarded his talents so highly that they wanted to turn him into a high-paid editor and thus put him on the path to more "important" jobs. But he was a rewrite man! He liked the challenge and excitement of it, and he liked the feelings of accomplishment his stellar work provided him. He refused promotion even when his bosses came close to demanding that he accept it.

Decades ago, the personality psychologist Robert White wrote a compelling paper about "The Concept of Competence" in which he argued that people yearn so strongly to feel competent or effective in dealing with their environment that competence could be thought of as a fundamental human need. This was apparently true for the rewrite man who had defined his life with work that was challenging and at the same time sure to leave him feeling competent.

White's theorizing suggests that there is a second important psychological need—beyond autonomy—that underlies intrinsically motivated behavior. People, impelled by the need to feel competent, might engage in various activities simply to expand their own sense of accomplishment. When you think about it, the curiosity of children—their intrinsic motivation to learn—might, to a large extent, be attributed to their need to feel effective or competent in dealing with their world.

At the Cobblestone Elementary School not far from the University of Rochester, the motivating power of the need to feel effective is right out in the open to be seen. The school is in a stark, brick structure, but it has an approach to education that begins with thinking about what the children need in order to learn and develop effectively. It is quite rare in this regard.

Outside the building that Cobblestone occupies there are no jungle gyms or elaborate playthings, but any visitor on any day will see young children having a fabulous time. Outdoors, seven- or eight-year-olds might be digging in the ground for fossils—or imaginary

fossils, anyway. Indoors, five-year-olds who cannot read might be
playing a board game, making up the rules as they go along.

All of this is not "unstructured" in the negative sense of children
being ignored or set free to do whatever they please. On the contrary,
guidance comes from teachers who encourage the children to reflect
on what they have been doing and from older children who set examples for the younger ones to emulate. The younger ones, of course,
are propelled by a desire to achieve, accomplish, and learn—by the
need for competence—and they are guided by elders who care about
the children's development. In these children, one sees intrinsic motivation joyfully at work—the tendency to explore and experiment,
the desire for novelty—and the need to feel competent is an important energizer.

The feeling of competence results when a person takes on and, in
his or her own view, meets optimal challenges. Optimal challenge is
a key concept here. Being able to do something that is trivially easy
does not lead to perceived competence, for the feeling of being effective occurs spontaneously only when one has worked toward accomplishment. Like the children at Cobblestone School, with their
spontaneous, inner desire to test themselves and the environment, all
of us are striving for mastery, for affirmations of our own competence. One does not have to be best or first, or to get an "A," to feel
competent; one need only take on a meaningful personal challenge
and give it one's best.

I f there really is an innate need for competence, then the feelings of
competence should affect people's intrinsic motivation. To test
this, I did a simple experiment in which I arranged for subjects in one
group to succeed relatively well at puzzle solving and those in another group to fail quite badly. I managed that by selecting puzzles
for the two groups that were quite different in difficulty level, even
though they appeared to be similar. As expected, those who received
evidence of their own competence were subsequently more intrinsi-

cally motivated than those who saw evidence of relative incompetence.

The fact that perceived competence is related to intrinsic motivation leads directly to a very important set of issues about giving people feedback. For example, does it help people's intrinsic motivation to praise their performance? Praise is an extrinsic reward, but it is a different sort of reward from the others that have been discussed so far. It's not tangible like money and it's not offered up front—you never hear someone say, "I'll praise you if you do such and such." Still, praise is widely used as a reward, and experts often encourage people to use praise as a motivator—at work, home, school, and throughout everyday life. People assume it works. They assume that if they praise someone for a worthy deed, it will make that person feel better and be more likely to engage in the desirable behavior again.

Wayne Cascio (now an industrial psychologist at the University of Colorado), Judith Krusell (now a clinical psychologist in New Jersey), and I did another simple experiment. We gave positive feedback—statements like, "Good, you solved that one faster than most people"—to half the subjects, but we gave no performance feedback to the other half. Because the task was one where people could not really tell how well they were doing, it was possible to give positive feedback that was believable no matter how well they actually did. Half the subjects in each experimental group were male and half female, and the results were quite startling indeed, so unexpected that, in a kind of scientific double take, we felt obliged to give the experiment another try. In both of these cases, the results indicated that praising males increased their intrinsic motivation, but praising females decreased their intrinsic motivation. It was apparently the case that females got "hooked" by the praise, whereas males, for whom it simply affirmed their success—it signified that they were competent—were propelled onward by it. But why might that be so?

Clearly, some consideration of the general social conditions of the time might help with an explanation. It was the mid 1970s, and one of the most pressing insights of that moment—although, of course, it seems rather familiar to say it now—was the realization of how men and women had been socialized differently throughout childhood. Boys were expected to be more adventurous, girls less so; boys were expected to be focused on success, girls on being interpersonally sensitive. Feminists, and many of the rest of us, believed then and now that females were getting the short end of the stick when it came to opportunities for achievement. Through the insidious messages in the social milieu, women were being taught that being competent at various tasks was not as important for them as for men, and, at the same time, they were developing a kind of hypersensitivity to praise because they had been taught to make praise a more central aspect of their human discourse. This hypersensitivity apparently led the women in the study to experience the praise as a control, and they quickly learned to see the puzzle solving as a way of obtaining praise rather than something that provides its own intrinsic gratification.

These results were, of course, provocative, prompting controversy and further experiments. Ryan, for example, wondering if all positive feedback would undermine the intrinsic motivation of females, decided to use two different sets of positive feedback, one set consisting of controlling statements (using words like "living up to expectations" and "doing as you should") and another set consisting of statements that were not at all controlling (no mention of shoulds or expectations and no social comparison information, just simple statements such as "you've done very well"). It turned out that the controlling praise decreased everyone's intrinsic motivation—males and females alike—whereas the noncontrolling praise left everyone's interest and persistence at a high level.

The point, then, is that praise can be clearly noncontrolling or clearly controlling, as Ryan's study showed. Or it can be somewhat ambiguous as was the case in the study I did with Cascio and Krusell. If it is noncontrolling, it will enhance people's intrinsic motivation; if it is controlling, it will diminish people's intrinsic motivation; and if it is ambiguous with respect to whether or not it is controlling, males and females may interpret it differently. Females seem to have a greater tendency than do males to experience it as controlling.

This research highlighted the fact that even praise when used as an interpersonal reward *can* have a negative effect on the enjoyment and motivation of people receiving it, and the problem once again is control. It is thus imperative, when using praise, to be careful about your own intentions. Are you praising in an attempt to get the person to do more? Are you perhaps being subtly controlling? With praise, with rewards, with limits, if you want to use them in a way that does not undermine intrinsic motivation, you have to take pains to minimize the controlling language, the controlling style, and your own agenda of controlling the other person's behavior.

Unfortunately, all too often, parents, coaches, or media commentators impose controlling external criteria, and they use feedback and rewards in evaluative and controlling ways. In order to motivate competent activity in their children or athletes, for example, people often become controlling and thus interfere with the natural motivation that was already there.

It is truly amazing how, in the Olympics, for example, commentators speak about the performance of someone who ends up taking the silver medal in, say, men's figure skating as if he were a disappointing failure. The second-best skater in the world, and he's treated like a loser. That's what happens when we turn everything into a contest in which there is only one winner, in which winning matters more than playing well or being a good sport. By creating highly controlling interpersonal contexts, we undermine the natural desire to feel competent.

Competition does not need to be treated that way. The real function of competition could be viewed as providing challenge—as providing an opportunity for people to test themselves and to improve—and in the process to have fun. The pressure to win is extra; it is something that has been added, and it is the added pressure that undermines intrinsic motivation, as was shown in the study by Reeve and myself reported in Chapter Three.

T he concept of perceived competence is employed by many so-
     cial and clinical psychologists these days, people such as Stan-
ford University psychologist Albert Bandura. They agree that the
important feeling of being effective is essential for a high level of
motivation, but they have failed to realize that perceived competence
must be accompanied by the experience of autonomy for the most
positive results. As people gain competence in dealing with themselves and their world, and as they become more autonomous in
doing that, they will perform more effectively and display a greater
sense of well-being. But gaining competence alone is not enough. To
be a competent pawn, to be effective but not to feel truly volitional
and self-determined at the activity you can do so well, does not promote intrinsic motivation and general well-being. Of course, the
worst case is to lack both perceived competence and perceived autonomy, which can easily result in a condition of ill-being such as
depression—a state so lacking in motivation that it can lead to de-
spair and even death—but perceived competence without perceived
autonomy has also been shown to have negative effects.

We see this problem in life all the time. For example, recognizing
the importance of competence, many adults give children challenges
and then pressure them to master the challenges. Especially, if a child
shows talent, the challenges can be great and the pressures intense.
But there are two problems in this approach, even if the adults are
well-meaning. First, if the challenge is not optimal—if it is not realistically within the child's grasp—it will not be motivating. And second, the challenge must be accompanied by autonomy support
rather than control to yield the best results. In fact, when adults are
autonomy supportive, they will almost surely provide optimal challenges, because being autonomy supportive involves taking the others' perspective. When people do that, they will understand what is
optimal for the others. Providing others with challenges that will
allow them to end up feeling both competent and autonomous, will
promote in them greater vitality, motivation, and well-being.

Autonomy fuels growth and health because it allows people to
experience themselves as themselves, as the initiators of their own

actions. Perceived competence, or mastery, without perceived autonomy is not enough because being a competent puppet does not nourish humanness. In such competence, the essence of life is missing.

The strivings for competence and autonomy together—propelled
by curiosity and interest—are thus complementary growth forces
that lead people to become increasingly accomplished and to go on
learning throughout their lifetimes. The research reported thus far,
along with more to come, indicates quite clearly that, on every level,
the person who feels competent and autonomous, who directs his or
her own life, is immeasurably better off than the person who does
not.

I f positive feedback *can* have a potentially deleterious effect on
motivation and performance by diminishing perceived autonomy,
what must be the case with negative feedback? The answer, of
course, is clear enough: It is far more disastrous. Experiments have
showed that, too. When people were told that they did not perform
well, they felt incompetent and controlled, and all their intrinsic motivation was drained away.

But just because negative feedback can have a demotivating effect does not mean that we, as parents, teachers, or managers should
simply ignore poor performance. With negative feedback, as with
rewards, limits, and positive feedback, it's all in how you do it.

I had a student once, a middle-aged woman pursuing her Ph.D.
in nursing, who supervised nursing students at the university's medical center. She raised a practical problem in class one day. It centered
on what to say to a young nurse who had made a mistake in hooking
up a man's intravenous tube—a mistake that resulted in an air bub-
ble getting into it. It was a potentially very serious matter, to be sure,
but fortunately her coworker noticed it and pointed it out so the man
was not harmed. "What," my student asked, "was the appropriate
thing to have said to this young woman about the incident?"

Another student in the class, a doctoral student in psychology,
answered, "You should point out to her what a serious mistake it

was, being sure she understands the potential consequences for the patient, and tell her that she really must be more careful in the future. Oh, and be sure to point out that you are not criticizing her, but instead are criticizing the behavior." Other students voiced their agreement with this approach.

What exactly was contained within those comments? Well, first, the students agreed it was important to step up to the problem—it is certainly not something to be ignored. Second, they advocated providing information about the possible consequences and the importance of being careful. And, third, they suggested phrasing the feedback in a way that focused on the behavior and not on the person. All three points are meaningful, and in the right situations could facilitate motivation. So, it would seem that they were right on target.

But let's stop and think about it for a moment. Imagine yourself in the position of the young nursing student. Do you suppose you would have realized it was a serious error with potentially dire consequences? Of course you would. And the admonition to be more careful would almost certainly have served no meaningful purpose. Could the young woman possibly not have known that she should be more careful?

So I asked the class, "How about starting by asking her what her thoughts were about the incident?" If we want to be autonomy supportive of the young trainee, we need to start from her perspective. And what better way to find out her perspective than to invite her to share it. "I'd be willing to bet," I went on, "that if you asked her, she would say everything you thought it necessary to say." In fact, she would probably go even further to criticize herself—as a nurse and as a person—which would not be helpful, so you might end up having to reassure her. But otherwise she could probably do most of the talking.

One of the heartening things you will find if you are truly autonomy supportive with trainees, subordinates, or anyone else you are teaching or supervising, is that those people will typically be amazingly accurate in evaluating their own performance. In many cases, they may be more accurate than you are. But just as surely, if you become controlling and evaluative with them, they will be defensive, evasive, and in all likelihood will blame others. Some will be highly self-deprecatory rather than pointing the finger at everyone else, but neither type of response will lead to productive problem solving and effective performance.

For the type of engagement that promotes optimal problem solving and performance, people need to be intrinsically motivated. That, as we have seen, begins with instrumentalities—with people understanding how to achieve desired outcomes—and with people feeling competent at the instrumental activities. Then, it is facilitated by interpersonal contexts that support people's autonomy. With these important ingredients, people will be likely to set their own goals, develop their own standards, monitor their own progress, and attain goals that benefit not only themselves, but also the groups and organizations to which they belong.

PART TWO

The Role of Interpersonal Connectedness

SIX

The Inner Force of Development

Psychology has a history that is a bit like a patient with a split personality. It has two identities, dramatically different, each off in its own sphere of research and influence. One emerged as the study of internal processes that are often difficult to observe directly. The other emerged with a single-minded focus on distinct behaviors. The former—the psychoanalytic tradition which began with Sigmund Freud's revolutionary work—was built on the belief that the reasons people act and feel as they do are deep within them. Thus change can be promoted only when people probe their psychic depths and bring into awareness those inner, often unconscious, dynamics. The latter—the empirical tradition which began as behaviorism—presumed that the causes of people's actions are the reinforcements they have received, so a person's life can be dramatically altered by precise adjustments in the administration of reinforcements.

Humanistic psychology—including the work of Carl Rogers, who pioneered client-centered therapy, and Fritz Perls, who pioneered Gestalt therapy—has evolved out of the psychoanalytic tradition. Although the differences between the psychoanalytic and humanistic perspectives are frequently discussed, the two actually share many features. Both understand human behavior in terms of motivational and emotional dynamics; both focus on promoting awareness as the basis for change; and both build theory using observations and direct experience.

Behavioral theory, within the empirical tradition, is something else altogether. It shares few features with psychoanalytic or humanistic psychologies. B. F. Skinner, its best-known proponent, emphasized that the science of psychology should focus on observable behaviors and the environmental conditions that reinforce them. According to the rules of science, before a phenomenon will be accepted as fact, it must be demonstrated reliably by different investigators. Keeping the focus on observable behaviors and environmental reinforcers, Skinner argued, would help to ensure replicability of behavioral phenomena.

Through the decades, the empirical tradition has also evolved. Many theorists now focus on individuals' thoughts, rather than just observable behaviors and environmental reinforcements. Behaviors are thus explained in terms of people's thoughts about reinforcements—their expectations and interpretations—rather than just the objective description of reinforcements themselves. Thus, many modern empirical psychologists—referred to as cognitive theorists— have moved "inside the person" to search for the causes of behavior, but they have stayed largely at the level of people's thoughts rather than going deeper to their motivations. Furthermore, modern empiricists have continued to view the person in mechanistic terms. Humans, they say, are information-processing machines that work like computers to solve problems, make decisions, and behave.

Psychology's two fascinatingly different identities take divergent approaches to discovering truth within the field of psychology. The psychodynamic approach bases its theory on clinical experiences, whereas the empirical approach employs statistical analyses of data collected from scientific experiments. Of course, each of these two traditions is well aware of the other, but their attitudes toward each other range from benign neglect to vigorous contempt. Few psychologists have embraced the contributions of each to work toward a scientific study of psychological dynamics.

As I approached the study of intrinsic motivation, I was faced with the challenge of bringing together important aspects of these two traditions. I was determined to use empirical research methods, but the concept of intrinsic motivation did not seem as if it could be conveyed with mechanistic notions. Furthermore, I had the intuitive sense that intrinsic motivation was just one aspect of a larger set of phenomena that I really wanted to explore, and these phenomena would surely need a more humanistic starting point. What was needed was an empirical humanism.

T he influential child psychologist Jean Piaget observed that children seem to imbue everything with life. It is quite interesting that, in contrast to this anthropomorphic view held by children, many empirical psychologists hold just the opposite view, namely, that everything is inanimate. It is almost as if people, being mere machines like the computer, were dead.

The inanimate viewpoint, the assumption that life is lifeless, lends itself easily to empirical study and to behavioral and cognitive explanations of behavior. But one of the troubling things about this approach is that it leads directly to the depiction of human behavior as being governed by external forces that prod, coerce, seduce, and direct. In the same way that programmers control the behavior of computers, savvy motivators must be relied on to control the behavior of people.

A very different, but in a functional sense quite similar, view has been expressed by sociologist Talcott Parsons. He portrayed the birth of each infant as the invasion of a barbarian. People are alive, he would agree, but not in a constructive sense; they are alive but they are savages who need to be tamed. This infant-as-barbarian view is similar to the person-as-passive-mechanism view in the sense that both understand development as resulting from controlling children's behavior. Both assert that society must shape the person. Both suggest that socializing agents must create the *self* of the child. In short, both see development as something that must be *done to the child* by the social world.

If people are not machines waiting to be programmed, or savages waiting to be tamed, what then are they? They are *organisms* who, by their nature, explore, develop, and take on challenges, not because they are programmed to, not because they are forced to, but because it is in their nature to. Development, when viewed from this perspective, as Piaget and a few other pioneering psychologists, such as Heinz Werner, have done, is really quite a different matter. It is a more constructive matter, a more human matter. Development is not something done to the child by the social world, but, rather, it is something *the child does actively,* with the support and nourishment of the social world.

The assumption that human beings are organisms rather than mechanisms represents the humanistic starting point for the view of motivation employed by Richard Ryan and myself. Our agenda has thus been to ongoingly illuminate motivational phenomena by beginning with organismic, humanistic assumptions and employing empirical research methods.

At the heart of our perspective is the assertion that people develop through the process of organismic integration as they proactively engage their world. This means that there is a basic tendency within people to move toward greater coherence and integrity in the organization of their inner world. It means that inherent in the nature of human development is the movement toward greater consistency and harmony within.

The assertion that integration is the central feature of development has several ramifications. It encompasses the idea that people are inherently proactive and inclined to operate on their environment to bring about effects, and in the process to learn and to grow. That, of course, is simply another way of stating that people are intrinsically motivated. But also contained within the organismic integration principle is the idea that implicit within life itself is the tendency to move toward an ever more complex, yet organized, condition. Human development is a process in which organisms continually elaborate and refine their inner sense of themselves and their world in the service of greater coherence. The urge to develop an integrated sense of self is thus a central feature of who we are as individuals, and the activity—both physical and mental—that is necessary for this natural developmental trajectory is intrinsically motivated.

Concepts similar to what we call organismic integration can be found in other theories as well. Among Freud's more important contributions was his proposal of a synthetic function of the ego, which suggests that throughout life, people work to bring coherence to their experience, and, indeed, to the development of their own personality. It was a proposal much like Piaget's hypothesized organizational principle, and much like the assertion by Rogers (and fellow humanistic psychologist Abraham Maslow) that there is an actualizing tendency within people, leading them toward greater internal harmony and integrity.

In a way, intrinsic motivation and organismic integration together can be thought of as a kind of *life force,* a postulate of an implicit directionality to development. It is this set of ideas that Ryan and I, working with our various colleagues, have been studying using empirical methods. The experiments on intrinsic motivation represent the initial phase of that exploration.

That research has indicated that intrinsic motivation is a viable concept; that intrinsically motivated performance is superior in many ways to externally controlled performance; and that social contexts that support and affirm people's perceived autonomy and perceived competence enhance intrinsic motivation, while social contexts that diminish people's perceived autonomy and perceived competence undermine intrinsic motivation.

Although each of the experiments discussed so far involved specific behaviors (and their relation to intrinsic motivation), when considered together they begin to speak to the broader issue of human development. In other words, they can be thought of as being directly related to the conditions that nurture the human organism's energy and tendency toward integration in personality.

To get a clearer idea of what is meant by integration in personality, think of the football player who is also an artist and who is competent and content in both roles—a young man who has managed to belong to two different sorts of teams. To allow these varied aspects of himself to find expression, and to *feel like himself* as he expresses each, he would have to have fended off pressures to be one or the other—the powerful forces of stereotyping that would foist on him a false, less complex sense of who he is. The young man would need to have maintained intrinsic motivation for both as he developed a harmonious relation between these two parts of himself.

The development of integration in personality, of being who you truly are and becoming all you are capable of, is what allows authenticity. And this, of course, does not develop divorced from societal influences. The young artistic athlete (or athletic artist) was able to fend off pressures, no doubt, in part because he had support from one or more adults—parents, coaches, teachers—who were able to facilitate his autonomy and the integration of diverse aspects of his personality. By providing autonomy support, they would have facilitated the young man's natural development toward greater integration and authenticity.

When you hear the assertions that intrinsic motivation and the inherent integrative tendency are natural, you might immediately wonder why there seems to be so little proactivity and so little integration among the people you see every day. Why do so many of the children in our schools seem to be without vital energy and motivation to learn? Why do some seem driven only by fear of the next test or the desperate desire to avoid disapproval? And why do some behave like barbarians, sassing the teacher or tearing up the place?

Those, of course, are the very questions that our research has been addressing, and the results indicate that the innately striving and thriving organism—the human being—is vulnerable to being controlled and made to feel ineffective. Even in what might seem to some observers to be relatively benign circumstances—like relying on rewards to motivate performance, for example—a person's natural thrust toward growth can be seriously blunted. When that happens, the person begins to look more like the passive mechanism posited by many experimental psychologists, or like the barbarian that Talcott Parsons says we all are at heart.

As psychologists, Ryan and I frame this set of issues with the question: Why is there so much individual difference in the amount of integration and activity demonstrated by different people? That, of course, is one of the central questions that are addressed throughout this book, and the experiments and examples thus far reported provide part of the answer, which in essence is that different people have been exposed to different amounts of controlling, demotivating circumstances during their development.

To characterize our perspective more formally, we view human behavior and experience in terms of the dialectic between the person and the environment—the interaction (and potential opposition) between the active organism striving for unity and autonomy and the social context that can be either nurturing of or antagonistic toward the person's organismic tendencies. Synthesis occurs when there is enough support in the social context so that the natural, proactive tendencies are able to flourish. But in the absence of adequate supports, not only will intrinsic motivation be undermined, but so too will the development of a more integrated or coherent sense of self.

There are two main types of contexts that can turn a vital life into a disaffected one. The first and more obvious is the type referred to in the discussion of Bulgaria. Social contexts that are extremely inconsistent or chaotic, that make it impossible for people to figure out what is expected of them and how to behave competently so as to achieve intrinsic or extrinsic outcomes, will lead to a general thwarting of the human spirit. It will leave people with little or no motivation. We say it produces amotivation. The second and less obvious is the type that has been the primary focus of this book—namely, controlling environments that demand, pressure, prod, and cajole people to behave, think, or feel in particular ways. These are the environments that promote automatons—people who engage in instrumental reasoning, comply with demands, are, in a sense, only half alive, and, once in a while, are prompted to defy the controls.

It is truly amazing, as pointed up by our findings, that if people are ongoingly treated as if they were either passive mechanisms or barbarians needing to be controlled, they will begin to act more and more that way. As they are controlled, for example, they are likely to act more and more as if they need to be controlled. That fact has led some commentators to conclude that society should use more controls. It has led to the call for greater discipline, for more heavy-handedness. But ironically, it should call for just the opposite. This phenomenon behooves us to insist even more emphatically that it is time to stop looking for the easy answers contained in the reliance on control and instead to start employing more autonomy-supportive approaches.

The importance of autonomy support for human development has been confirmed for Ryan and myself not only by our research, but by our clinical work as well. One such example is a case involving a young woman I'll call Stephanie. She had experienced a good deal of emotional pain in her childhood, particularly surrounding the loss of her mother who had fled with a lover, leaving eleven-year-old Stephanie and her father to fend for themselves. Despite that kind of harsh stress, Stephanie did manage to do well enough in school to gain entry to a nursing program at a top university. Once there, however, personal difficulties began to surface in an alarming way. Her friends noticed that she had become awfully thin and that she related to food strangely, scraping the cheese off her pizza, for example. And she always ate her salad without dressing, taking extreme measures to cut down on calories despite the fact that she was unsettlingly thin already. Her friends were caring enough and aware enough to insist that Stephanie see someone at an eating-disorders clinic. Stephanie, at this point, weighed barely one hundred pounds.

The diagnosis, of course, was anorexia nervosa, and the program of action at the clinic was clear-cut. The clinicians' goal was to alter her eating habits through behavior modification. Targets for eating were set up, a specified number of calories had to be taken in, and a prescribed progression of weight gain was established. She was to record everything she ate, and if her weight fell to ninety-five pounds, she would be put on a more drastic regimen. Stephanie had to sign a contract, indicating her agreement with this plan.

The approach was pure control. Undesirable behaviors were identified, and a controlling program was devised to replace them with desirable behaviors. She was told that she had to demonstrate improvement if she wished to avoid even more stringent control of her life. This latter element of the plan was intended to give added strength to the treatment. She would eat more, it was reasoned, in order to avoid the consequence of more stringent control.

But Stephanie never did gain the targeted weight while she was in that treatment. Her diary showed that she was adhering to the eating requirements, but she frustrated her clinicians' efforts by slipping to the limit of ninety-five pounds (and even that was, as it turned out, an inflated figure because Stephanie cleverly had taken to drinking large quantities of water to bloat herself each time she was to go to the clinic for her examination). The tension built, and Stephanie eventually withdrew from treatment.

A few months later, one of Stephanie's friends suggested she might want to talk with Ryan. His approach, of course, was very different. He was less concerned with the specific maladaptive behaviors than with what was actually going on inside Stephanie— the psychodynamic aspects of her condition. He listened to her with great care, trying to see the world from her point of view. What was she thinking or feeling each time she removed the cheese from a slice of pizza, for example? What was going on when she falsified her diary (which she quickly conceded she had done)?

Stephanie, he learned, felt that she was fat despite her emaciated state. Her hips, regardless of what anybody else might think, seemed to her to be offensively wide and her thighs seemed grossly heavy. But the interesting thing about it is that these perceptions of her body emerged only when she felt inadequate, criticized, or judged. As treatment progressed, Stephanie was gradually able to draw a connection between her painful vulnerability and the events of being abandoned by her mother and overly controlled by her father, who did his best with her but was obviously overwhelmed by the task of raising a teenage daughter by himself.

The well-meaning therapists in the clinic who had attempted to change her ways through behavior modification had inadvertently become part of the very dynamics that had already affected her adversely. The lack of empathic listening was stimulative of her mother's absence, and the controlling methods were reminiscent of the strained aspects of her relationship with her father.

In Ryan's therapy sessions with Stephanie, he never made the eating disorder a focus of the discussions. But she was, as you might guess, quite preoccupied by it and brought it up on her own. And when she did, she was able to see how her feelings of inadequacy led directly to her serious eating problem. As these dynamics became clearer, she no longer felt that she had to control her body so severely. The experience of an autonomy-supportive listener had helped Stephanie's natural developmental process to get back on track.

Repeatedly, the experiments have shown and I have emphasized that people need to feel competent and autonomous for intrinsic motivation to be maintained and, I now argue, for development to proceed naturally. Before moving on to address the developmental issues more directly and discuss the developmental research, I want to emphasize the point that, when it comes to competence and autonomy, it's really the person's own perceptions that matter. To be intrinsically motivated people need to *perceive themselves* as competent and autonomous; they need to feel that they are effective and self-determining. Someone else's opinion does not do the trick.

People's perceptions of competence (or incompetence) are often quite closely linked to their actual performance at some target activity. When people succeed at an activity, the research shows that they are likely to perceive themselves to be more competent. The same is true when they win a competition and when they receive positive feedback. Still, their perceptions do not always match up with the objective data. Just as Stephanie perceived herself to be heavy when, in fact, she was extremely thin, people who are actually doing well at an activity (in school, say) may perceive themselves to be quite inadequate. When this occurs, there is clearly some emotional process at play, and because the link between performance and perceived competence is so direct, the discrepancy can typically be detected quite easily. With perceived autonomy, the issue is somewhat trickier.

The key to whether people are living autonomously is whether they feel, deep within themselves, that their actions are their own choice. It is a psychological state of feeling free, and it is in the eye of the behaver, so to speak. But it requires that people take an honest look. It is quite possible for people to report feeling free, and even to "sort of" believe it, while deluding themselves. Of course, when that is the case, people will not exhibit the qualities typically associated with perceived autonomy.

Because the issue of autonomous action, and thus integrated development, concerns people's own experience of their behavior, the issues may sound mysterious and elusive. But surely it is true that we can all feel within ourselves, at least intuitively, if we are autonomous. We can know (if it interests us to know) when our actions are self-initiated or self-endorsed; we can know when we are interested, engaged, and alive. There is a feeling of harmony, a feeling of emotional integration, with the different aspects of the self working in contented partnership, even if the self in question is out of sync with society's expectations.

And just as surely, we know when we are being controlled. A woman who attempts to stop smoking just to please her doctor, or because her coworkers have subtly criticized her, would know, if she were willing to listen to her internal voice, that she is not being autonomous in her efforts. And a man who stayed out late because his wife insisted that he come home early would know, if he were willing to be honest with himself, that he was not acting freely. When people are either complying with or defying controls, they are not being autonomous, and they can know that.

Naturally, there will be times when people are not willing to be honest with themselves, when they engage in self-deception and insist they truly want to do something that they are actually doing out of obligation or fear. But even then, they may have an inkling that something is not quite right, and that inkling can provide the cue to look deeper. They will sense the inner tension and notice how insistent they are being. They will become suspicious because they know what it means when they "doth protest too much." Sensitive onlookers may also be able to pick it up because the people will likely be rigid and devoid of their natural vitality.

C arl Rogers became rhapsodic when he described the psychologically free or "fully functioning" person. Such an individual, Rogers said, "is completely engaged in the process of becoming himself, and thus discovers that he is soundly and realistically social. . . ." Rogers was pointing to what Ryan and I regard as a third, innate psychological need. People not only need to be effective and free; they also need to feel connected with others in the midst of being effective and autonomous. We call it the need for relatedness— the need to love and be loved, to care and be cared for.

Early motivation theorists focused on the sex drive (which is, there can be no doubt, an important motivator), but in so doing, they neglected what may be an even more important motivator of ongoing human activity: the psychological desire for relatedness. One even suspects that much sexual activity may have more to do with the urge to feel loved, to feel included, to feel related, than it does with the drive for sexual gratification.

People have often portrayed the needs for autonomy and relatedness as being implicitly contradictory. You have to give up your autonomy, they say, to be related to others. But that is simply a misportrayal of the human being. Part of the confusion stems from equating autonomy and independence, which are in fact very different concepts.

Independence means to do for yourself, to *not* rely on others for personal nourishment and emotional support. Autonomy, in contrast, means to act freely, with a sense of volition and choice. It is thus possible for a person to be independent and autonomous (i.e., to freely not rely on others), or to be independent and controlled (i.e., to feel forced not to rely on others). Consider these examples.

Although I've not seen him in years, I had a friend in California who was a fisherman. He kept his small boat near Monterey, and each day (weather permitting) he would leave the harbor about 6:30 a.m. He would be alone in his small boat for the next ten or twelve hours, and he told me that he felt a sense of peace and contentment surrounded by the power of the ocean, the sensations of nature, and the test of himself against the fish, the waves, and, if I recall correctly, the divine forces. Of course, he was not wholly "an island unto himself"—he had a wife and children whom he loved very much, and I too felt quite close to him when I used to see him—but he was a good example of a person who was both autonomous and relatively independent. He *chose* to spend a great deal of time alone, relying on himself.

Although my fisherman friend was a good example of autonomous independence, most of the people I've known who were highly independent were *driven* to that independence by inner or outer forces. Their independence—or emotional isolation—was controlled; it was not a choice. I am thinking of another individual, who never had someone to rely on or trust when he was young. He was pushed by his unreliable parents to be independent—to stand on his own and be strong. "Never trust anyone," his parents told him, but really it was their actions more than their words that led him to develop a mistrust of others and as a result to remain highly independent. Throughout his life he has had casual friends, but he has never been able to develop a deep, personal connection with anyone.

The converse of independence is dependence, which means to rely on others for interpersonal support. People are naturally inclined to form emotional bonds with others and then to both rely on and provide for those others. Dependence is motivated by the need for relatedness. It is intertwined with love, and feeling autonomously dependent is natural, useful, and healthy.

Just as independence can coexist with either autonomy or control, dependence can also coexist with either. Autonomous dependence is in fact a quite natural state. Coerced or controlled dependence—dependence that is not truly chosen—is what's maladaptive. Dependence has often been given a bum rap in our society, which tends to fetishize independence, but people have needs for both autonomy and relatedness, so the combination of the two, which results in an optimal amount of dependence, should have quite positive correlates.

To test this out, Ryan collaborated with graduate student John Lynch on a study exploring the issue of independence and autonomy in teenagers. High school is a time when adolescents struggle to achieve a certain level of independence from their parents, and many writers have maintained that relinquishing family attachments is a critical task during this developmental phase. Ryan and Lynch found, however, that a willing or volitional dependence on parents (rather than a strong independence from them) was essential for the teenagers' integrity and well-being. Of course, people vary in how much dependence is appropriate for them (recall my fisherman friend), but so long as they are autonomous with regard to their dependence they will find the appropriate amount for themselves.

SEVEN

When Society Beckons

I visited a hardware store not long ago to pick up a small piece of pipe. I found one that looked right, but I needed to know the diameter, so I hailed a salesman—a pleasant young man of about eighteen—and asked him for help. Quite agreeably he took his tape measure and held it up to the pipe. He looked at the ruler for a moment and then he looked at me. "What's the mark just below the half-inch mark?" he asked. I was stunned, and it took me a moment to answer.

As I drove home with my piece of pipe—seven-sixteenths of an inch in diameter—the incident echoed in my mind. An apparently well-socialized young man, probably a high school graduate, still did not know his fractions. It seemed to me that familiarity with fractions would be useful for almost anyone, but especially for someone in a job that periodically calls for measuring things. What had happened, I wondered. Why hadn't he assimilated one of the most basic skills taught in school?

One reason might be that he did not find math interesting, that he was not intrinsically motivated to learn it. But here is a case where learning something would have been useful for this fellow even if he did not find it interesting. The incident raises the question of how to promote a desirable behavior such as learning fractions if the behavior is not intrinsically motivated—if the person does not find it interesting.

As socializing agents—parents, teachers, and managers—it is our job to encourage others to do many things they might find boring but that allow them to become effective members of society. Actually, our job goes beyond just encouraging them to do the activities; it's more challenging than that. *The real job involves facilitating their doing the activities of their own volition, at their own initiative, so they will go on doing the activities freely in the future when we are no longer there to prompt them.*

Until now, the discussion has focused on activities that are intrinsically motivating for people—activities that people are fully willing to do on their own, out of interest—and the evidence is clear that if people in one-up positions act to facilitate a sense of autonomy and competence in others whom they teach or supervise, those others will remain interested and energized. The problem now being considered is a different one, but it is one that most people in one-up positions encounter all the time. It is the problem of helping people function in society, where many important activities are not interesting. It is a problem that is essential for socialization.

This problem has been addressed by countless theorists and other observers through the years. Often the word they use to describe the specific process through which individuals take on the values of society is internalization. However, the analyses of internalization have varied greatly depending on the philosophical assumptions they begin with. One approach to internalization begins with the view that people are either passive or barbarous—a view described in the previous chapter. The formulation of internalization from this perspective is essentially one of exerting external controls to program people's behavior. This is the perspective that sees socialization as something that gets done to people—as a matter of writing people's life scripts, of molding them into their rightful place in society.

Our approach, in contrast, holds that humans are imbued with the tendency and energy to grow and develop in accord with their psychological needs. This second approach views internalization as a proactive process in which the developing child *transforms* external prompts into internal prompts. Think of the boy who, over time, transformed requests from his parents to take out the garbage into a process where he keeps his eye on the garbage and takes it out when appropriate, no longer requiring parental prodding. The boy would have internalized a regulation.

When understood in this way, internalization was not something done *to* the boy (his parents did not program him); it was something done *by* the boy, with the help of his caregivers. The boy accepted the responsibility that his parents had requested of him. Of course, socializing agents play an important role in facilitating children's internalization, or thwarting it, but they do not do it. The children do.

This may at first seem to you like nothing but an issue of semantics, like nothing but facile jargon. It is, however, much more than that. From a psychological perspective it is more than that because it says a great deal about the nature of human development; and from a practical perspective, it is also much more because it leads to very different prescriptions about how to promote responsibility in our children, students, employees, patients, and citizens.

Internalization of a regulation and the value underlying it represents an instance of people's general propensity to integrate aspects of their world into an ever expanding and ever more unified representation of who they are—it is an instance of what we call organismic integration. In the taking-out-the-garbage example, the underlying value is the sharing of responsibility for making the family's life operate smoothly, and integration is the process through which that value became part of the child's developing self.

To be connected to and involved with others—that is, to satisfy the need for relatedness—children make accommodations, and they are naturally inclined to accept values and rules of their immediate groups, and of society. Through making such accommodations—through internalizing values and behavioral regulations—children learn to competently negotiate the social terrain. But it is important to realize that there are two quite different types of internalization, so merely internalizing regulations does not guarantee autonomous or authentic self-regulation.

The two forms of internalization are: introjection, which Fritz Perls likened to swallowing a rule whole rather than digesting it; and integration, which involves "digestion" and is the optimal form of internalization. To hold a rigid rule that pushes you around—that declares, demands, and demeans—and to act in accord with that rigid rule means that the rule has only been introjected, so it does not form the basis for truly autonomous performance of the activity. Autonomous functioning requires that an internalized regulation be accepted as your own; the regulation must become part of who you are. It must be integrated with your self. Through integration, people become willing to accept responsibility for activities that are important but not interesting—activities that are not intrinsically motivating.

People's need for autonomy, their need to be a causal agent in managing themselves, provides the energy for integrating (rather than just introjecting) a regulation. Thus, although the needs for relatedness and competence can motivate introjection, it is the need for autonomy that champions the integration of a value or regulatory process into one's *self*.

People often take in the values and rules of groups to which they belong, and they subsequently act accordingly. When this process occurs only incompletely, it results in introjects—that is, in internalizations that take the form of "shoulds" and "oughts." Introjects are voices in one's head, so to speak, that come from the outside and issue orders—sometimes like mean-spirited drill sergeants and sometimes like loving and well-meaning (but nonetheless intrusive) aunts. When internalizations become integrated, when they become true aspects of who one is, they allow more authentic actions and interactions.

If a young man who took over his dad's business were successful in integrating the experience, he would be autonomous in his career pursuit. He would do it with a true sense of choice, and he would not feel coerced. But think of what happens when this process goes awry, when partial digestion results in a pelting cascade of shoulds and oughts. There are various possible outcomes. The first of these is rigid, dutiful compliance. The best-selling author Michael Crichton represented an example of this at one point in his life. As he told the story to an interviewer, he had studied for many years to become a doctor, a goal that pleased his family very much. They evidently thought that growing up to be a doctor was exactly the right thing for him to do, the thing Crichton ought to do, and for many years Crichton himself bought into the plan. But after all that training he chose not to practice the profession. Instead, he did what he really wanted to do, which was to write. This decision, he told the interviewer, horrified his family.

Of course, I know neither Crichton nor his family, but, on the surface, this seems to be a case where the shoulds and oughts drove a highly capable young man to spend a large block of time preparing for a career in which he had little interest—a block of time during which he was controlled by strong introjects that led him to devote intense energy to learning medicine. Fortunately for him, he was able to free himself from those introjects and move on to the career he wanted. But in the more common scenario, people are held in the grip of introjects throughout their lifetime.

A second possible response to a panoply of introjects occurs when they do not have quite such a firm hold on a person. The result would be a kind of halfhearted adherence. Someone told me the story of a young man who did take over his family's business but was not integrated with respect to it. He did it because he thought he should, but he really felt emasculated in the process. This led to his running the business with the kind of ambivalence that ultimately led to its failure. He whined and complained about how things were going, coming up with a million excuses for why things were going badly, but he stuck with it, because he could not free himself from the introjects. They had a grip on him strong enough to keep him in the business, but not strong enough to make him committed to it.

A third possibility is that the person's tendency to defy could take over and lead to outright rebellion. Everyone knows a lawyer's son who not only does not become an attorney, even though there is pressure to do so, but instead gets himself into trouble with the law.

And there is the minister's daughter who becomes a vocal, dyed-in-the-wool atheist. In these cases, in all likelihood, what we would be witnessing are instances where the parents' values were introjected, but the children responded defiantly, as if to say to the introjects (and to their parents who initially pressured them), "You cannot control me; I'll show you who's in charge here!"

Introjected values and regulations can thus result in a variety of outcomes, but none of these is optimal. Clearly the halfheartedness and the rebellion are good for neither party. And while the rigid compliance may please the socializing agents who prompted it, there are serious costs to be borne by the people who comply.

In one study at the University of Rochester, Richard Ryan and Wendy Grolnick assessed the extent to which elementary-school children were motivated to do their schoolwork by introjected values and regulations, or alternatively, by more integrated ones. They also asked the teachers of these students to rate how motivated each student was, and they asked the children themselves how hard they tried to do well in school. In terms of how motivated the students appeared to the teachers, or how hard they tried to do well, it did not matter whether the children were more introjected or more integrated. Students with high levels of introjected regulation were seen by teachers as very motivated, and students with equally high levels of the more integrated form of regulation were also seen as highly motivated. And both types of children reported trying hard. But that's where the similarities ended. Those students who were more introjected were extremely anxious about school and displayed maladaptive patterns of coping with failure, whereas those who were more integrated enjoyed school and evidenced healthier patterns of coping when their efforts went awry.

How often must it be the case that we look at children and see that they are compliantly doing their schoolwork, or their chores, or whatever. "Ah," we say to ourselves, "they are highly motivated," and we think all is well. But maybe we should take another look and ask ourselves whether they are really doing it of their own volition, whether they are doing it with a sense of personal endorsement. If they are, all probably is well. But they may instead be introjected, working hard because they think they should and think they will gain approval by doing so. If so, these children may be hurting deep inside. The internal pressure to perform, which may look so good at first glance, will extract a significant price.

The compliance of these youngsters can work against them in various ways. Of course they will lack the vitality and enthusiasm that makes school a joyful experience, but an even sadder outcome is that it gets them focused on trying to please others rather than finding out what is right for themselves. Furthermore, in classrooms, these quiet, compliant students are often considered model students, so they are ignored—successful cases that need little attention. (Those who are noisy and defiant, in contrast, get a great deal of attention.) It may be a tragedy that these compliant students command so little attention, for the feelings they may hold deep within themselves—feelings of inadequacy, for example—deserve concern. These feelings can easily result from partial internalization—from introjection rather than integration—for when people introject rules and evaluations, they often feel that they cannot live up to them no matter how hard they try.

Introjecting rigid rules represents but one kind of failure of the internalization process to function effectively. Another, more extreme kind is not taking in values and regulations at all. The young salesman I encountered in the hardware store represents an example, trivial though it be, of a person failing to internalize a value and regulation—in his case, the value and regulation for mastering his fractions. A similar example is what seems to me to be a fairly widespread tendency not to value the use of traditionally correct language. I recently saw a brief autobiographical statement written by a thirty-year-old man who had graduated from a quite respectable university and went on to earn an MBA. The statement, which was part of a job application, began, "When I was young, me and my family lived in a small town." I thought it a shame that he hadn't learned the difference between the nominative and objective.

Although this too may be a relatively trivial matter, there are far more troubling ones. Think of the teenage girls who, having failed to internalize the value of formal education and the importance of having a means to support themselves, get pregnant so they'll have "something to care about." Their desire to be mothers is wonderful, but their becoming mothers before they can care for themselves and their children is not.

The question of why so many people appear not to have internalized values and regulations that are conducive to a productive, healthy life is an interesting and important one. How can this be, if, as I suggested, people are naturally motivated to internalize aspects of their social world that are useful for effective functioning? In other words, why do so many people fail to become willing to do activities that are good for them? To understand this seeming paradox, we must go back to the dialectic—the interaction between the active organism and the social context that can either support or thwart what the organism would be inclined to do naturally.

If you put a rooted avocado pit in a pot of earth it will probably grow into a tree, because it is in the nature of avocados to do that. It happens naturally. But not all pits become trees; some shrivel and decompose. They fail to thrive because the climate is inadequate, or the necessary nutrients are lacking. They need sun; they need water; and they need the right temperatures. Those elements do not *make* trees grow, but they are the nutriments that the developing avocados need, that are necessary in order for the avocados to do what they do naturally.

In the same way, developing human beings need psychological nutriments to do what they do naturally. To internalize and integrate aspects of society that are important for their own success in life within that society, they must experience satisfaction of their basic psychological needs—for autonomy, competence, and relatedness—

within the social context that provides the structures to be internalized.

A ll children face the challenge of responding to society's beckon-
ing without being overwhelmed or suffocated by it. They must
find a way to become related to the social world while also achieving
a sense of integrity within themselves. To a great extent, whether
these young people are successful in their attempts to be authentic
and responsible depends on the quality of their socializing environment. It depends on whether the socializing environment provides
the nutriments they need. It depends on whether the socializing environment allows them to satisfy their psychological needs while internalizing the values and regulations in question.

Part of the research program on internalization conducted by
Grolnick and Ryan explored the qualities of family life that promote
effective integration of external values and regulations. The researchers did structured interviews with the parents of elementary-
school children in a demographically diverse rural community. They
interviewed each parent separately, in the family's home. They went
into mobile homes propped on posts and sandwiched between others
just like them; into large freshly painted Victorian houses with fancy,
gleaming white gingerbread; into small, dilapidated farmhouses with
chickens and rusting truck chassis in the yard. In each case, the inter-
viewers asked a series of questions, such as what the parents do with
respect to their children's homework, and how they deal with the
often thorny issue of their children's household chores.

Grolnick and Ryan were interested in two main things: the extent to which parents support their children's autonomy, as opposed
to pressuring and controlling the children's behavior; and the extent
to which the parents were really involved—devoting time and attention to working with their children on these issues. The researchers
found all kinds of parents: some seemed to ignore their children and
hope for the best; some were demanding and critical; some were

smothering; and some were encouraging without being intrusive or demeaning.

The researchers also went into the local school to collect data from the children. Of primary interest was the degree to which the children had internalized the value of school—of doing homework and trying to do well at their school activities. Sure enough, those children whose parents were autonomy supportive and involved with them—who talked with them about their schoolwork and helped them with problems when they arose—had internalized the value quite well. These children believed schoolwork was important, and they accepted more responsibility for doing it.

Furthermore, with the greater internalization and integration came greater achievement and better adjustment. Through the internalization of the value of doing well in school (and of lending a hand around the house), these young people became more responsible and displayed greater well-being. It is particularly interesting that autonomy support, which was a crucial contextual nutriment for individuals' maintaining intrinsic motivation and as a result being more creative, processing information more deeply, and enjoying their activities more, also turns out to be essential for promoting internalization and integration of the motivation for uninteresting, though important, activities.

At one level of analysis, autonomy support means to relate to others—our children, students, and employees—as *human beings,* as active agents who are worthy of support, rather than as *objects* to be manipulated for our own gratification. That means taking their perspective and seeing the world from their point of view as we relate to them. Of course, autonomy support may require more work, but then, as socializing agents, that is our responsibility. For us to expect responsibility from others, we must accept our own responsibility as the agents of their socialization.

Although the concept of supporting autonomy to promote integration is rather abstract, it can be translated into concrete suggestions for socializing agents. In order to do that, I decided to run an experiment with the help of graduate students Haleh Eghrari, Brian

Patrick, and Dean Leone. We involved a group of experimental subjects in a highly uninteresting task of watching a computer screen for
the appearance of small spots of light. We hypothesized that three
specific aspects of how we presented the task would be important for
promoting integration.

First, providing a rationale for doing the uninteresting activity
seemed necessary. When you ask your child to pick up the toys on
the floor, for example, you might explain that the reason is so that
the toys won't get stepped on and broken, or so that the pieces won't
get lost. In the experiment, our rationale for asking subjects to do the
vigilance task was so that they could improve their concentration; it
is, after all, a task much like the ones used for training air-traffic
controllers. Second, it seemed important to acknowledge that people
might not want to do what they were being asked to do. This acknowledging people's feelings, you might recall, was also key in the
study where Koestner, Ryan, and their colleagues set limits to encourage children to be neat, and it worked to keep the limits from
undermining their intrinsic motivation. Here, we expected it to help
the subjects integrate the regulation of the uninteresting behavior.
Finally, we thought it essential that the language and style we used to
initiate participation in the activity involve minimal pressure. The
request should be more like an invitation than a demand, emphasizing choice rather than control.

We set up the experiment so these various experimenter behaviors—providing a rationale, acknowledging feelings, and minimizing
pressure—were either present or absent. And these factors did, in
fact, make a real difference. Each of the three behaviors contributed
to the amount of internalization that occurred: When they were present, there was more internalization than when they were absent. Internalization was manifest by subjects returning to the task
later—spending their subsequent free-choice time working on this
task rather than doing something else like reading magazines.

There was another, even more important, finding, however. It
turned out that if people internalized a regulation when the autonomy-supportive behaviors (the rationale, acknowledgment, and

choice) had been present, the subjects *integrated* the regulation. This was evident to us because their subsequent behavior was accompanied by their feeling free, enjoying the task, and believing that it was personally important. They were doing the behavior with a real sense of volition.

In contrast, if the internalization occurred in the controlling context, with the three important facilitating behaviors absent—and there was some, though considerably less than in the autonomy-supportive context—it took the form of *introjection,* not integration. These people, if they subsequently did the behavior, did it in spite of not feeling free, not enjoying it, and not believing it was personally important. They had swallowed the thought that they *should* do it, and they plodded forward, rather like sheep to slaughter.

The finding that controlling contexts prompted some internalization, even though less than autonomy-supportive ones, was important because it allowed us to reconcile reports by other, more behaviorally oriented psychologists that people can be "socialized" by controlling forces. It does appear that control can produce some internalization, but there will be less internalization under the controlling conditions than under autonomy-supportive ones, and furthermore the internalization that does occur will be only partial internalization—it will be only introjection.

An onlooker might very well describe people who have introjected regulations as being responsible and doing the right thing—just as the teachers in the Grolnick and Ryan research described their introjected students as motivated. But these people whose responsible behavior results from introjection pay the price of living with the unpleasant feelings and other negative consequences that accompany this type of internalization. Because there is an alternative—namely, responsible behaviors resulting from integration—that is not only more humane but more effective, it seems important that we work to promote integration rather than impose the strict discipline that promotes introjection and has significant psychological costs for the people being socialized.

The intrinsic need for relatedness leads people to be part of groups—initially their nuclear family, then larger groups, then society, and finally (one hopes) the global community—and this need, for good and for bad, opens people up to being socialized. When people belong to a group, the group becomes part of their identity, and they are naturally inclined to accept the group's values and mores. To a significant extent, this is the process through which responsibility develops.

Ryan and I put stock in the humanistic belief that it is important to be authentic, to be oneself, to march to one's own drummer. But just as obviously, we put stock in the importance of being responsible. To advocate autonomy does not mean to call for self-indulgence, because *being truly oneself* involves accepting responsibility for the well-being of others. The need to feel related leads people naturally to take on and assimilate aspects of the culture that can result in their making fertile contributions, and autonomy support from significant others helps this to occur. Individuals' need for relatedness, coupled with socializing agents' autonomy support, thus leads people to become responsible as they are becoming truly free. That is what being socialized means, at least in the positive and healthy sense of that term.

Because being true to oneself has often been equated with the egoistic doing of one's own thing, authenticity has often been perversely interpreted as justification for irresponsibility and then attacked by the critics who so interpret it. The selfish, egoistic doing of one's own thing is in fact irresponsible and may have demonstrably negative consequences. But those behaviors are not authentic; they are not expressions of human autonomy; they are not instances of being one's *true self*.

Writers who have decried the call for authenticity have, in their own way, acted irresponsibly. In the name of responsibility, they have called for the very control that is detrimental to human development, and thus to responsibility. Allan Bloom, for example, in *Closing of the American Mind,* wrote the following: "We are told, the healthy inner-directed person will *really* care for others. To which I can only respond: If you believe that, you can believe anything." Because Bloom's portrayal of authenticity was superficial and inaccurate—because he failed to recognize the important and complementary human needs for autonomy and relatedness—his discussion only adds confusion to a consideration of these issues.

People who have become selfish, narcissistic, or rebellious will not "care for others" and will act irresponsibly. These conditions come from failures to satisfy their basic needs for autonomy and relatedness. They are responses to caregiving that is cold and controlling or chaotic and permissive. In such environments, people will fail to become authentic, and they will fail to become responsible.

It cannot be emphasized enough that autonomy support is not the same thing as permissiveness. Still, people often interpret the idea of autonomy support as letting others get away with whatever they want. I recall one day when I was drinking coffee with a friend in the family room of his suburban Philadelphia home. His daughter Becky, who must have been about three, walked in from the backyard carrying a rubber ball. "Becky," he said, "leave the ball outdoors." Becky kept walking as if she hadn't heard a word. "Becky, *please* leave the ball outdoors," said her father, and Becky kept walking. My friend turned to me and resumed our conversation. I was aghast.

My friend was not being autonomy supportive; he was being permissive. He was failing to set limits and failing to be consistent in administering consequences. As a result, not only did he not get the behavior he desired (leaving the ball outside) but he was interfering with internalization and socialization. If there are no limits, no structures, no regulations to internalize, there will be no internalization.

Permissiveness is easy, but autonomy support is hard work. It requires being clear, being consistent, setting limits in an understanding, empathic way. Once, after I had lectured on the topic, a woman protested, "Autonomy support is very nice, but it's not always fair."

Unsure of what she meant, I encouraged her to say more. "Well," she said, "I had a very important business meeting last week and my baby-sitter didn't show up on time, so I was late for my meeting. He's a painter, and when I called to see where he was, he said, 'I'm right in the middle of a painting and I can't leave it now.' " Developing her argument, the woman said to me, "You're telling me I should have supported his autonomy and encouraged his self-expression. But it was very upsetting to me, and it's just not fair."

I agreed with her. It was not fair. And I added that if I were she I would probably not ask him to baby-sit again. It's great that he's a painter, and I would like to support his intrinsic motivation and creativity. But he made an agreement, and he was irresponsible in not following through. Trying to control him—that is, getting caught up in a power struggle—would surely be of no help. But if he cannot be counted on, if he does not keep his agreements, the consequence of his actions would be my not asking him back. Allowing him to be irresponsible and then asking him to baby-sit again is equivalent to being permissive. It is *not* autonomy support.

Many people think the only alternative to permissiveness is control—that is, heavy-handedness aimed at getting the other person to comply. Frequently, children make mistakes; sometimes they are irresponsible. But neither permissiveness nor cracking down produces optimal results. Instead, helping children master difficult situations and develop in healthy ways requires being autonomy supportive, which begins by understanding what is going on for them. We need to set limits and to be consistent in administering consequences, but it is important to do that with an understanding of the children.

There may be more to another's behavior than meets the eye. Maybe a daughter's noncooperation is a way of getting back at her parents for something. Maybe a son's acting out is a way of getting his parents' attention. There are many possibilities, and neither ignoring the behaviors nor becoming punitive is the answer. Understanding what they are feeling and needing, and at the same time being clear about the limits and consequences, is the route both to appropriate behavior and to the children's becoming better self-regulators.

There will be times in life when being a responsible parent, teacher, or manager requires sacrificing something that one would like in order to be autonomy supportive with a child, student, or employee. A mother, for example, might have been planning for weeks to go to a special concert on Saturday night, only to find out when Saturday arrives, that her young daughter is quite sick, or perhaps is very upset from a terrifying experience and needs comfort. Staying home is the responsible thing to do—even though it may seem unfair.

Most people will make sacrifices for the sake of a sick or frightened child. But being autonomy supportive may also require sacrifices that come less easily. To take an example: Suppose a father has a plan for the family to attend a big family gathering. On that day, his son has an important Little League game, and he doesn't want to let his teammates down. Both events are important, but the youngster prefers to be with his friends. His desire is a worthy one, it is an expression of himself as well as a genuine recognition of his responsibility as a member of the team. For the father to allow his son a choice, even though it means not having all the family together with the relatives, would be decidedly autonomy supportive. It is not permissive, though it may be a bit awkward, and it may deny the father what he wants.

A still more difficult situation is one where a child has been irresponsible. Suppose a son broke his mother's malachite armadillo after having been asked not to touch it. Autonomy support is still the route to go. That means that the mother would understand her son's point of view, and she would also administer consequences in a straightforward way—not to punish, not to control, but to follow through on the agreement (whether implicit or explicit) that was established when she asked him not to touch her armadillo. Being autonomy supportive means that the mother would administer consequences, but she would also hang in there with her son, trying to understand his perspective and helping him understand hers.

It may seem as though I'm singing a different tune—offering a different prescription—for the irresponsible baby-sitter and the irresponsible son. To the extent that I am, it is because the two situations are different. In both cases, administering consequences is important. But in the case of the son, it is important to work with him to facilitate his developing greater responsibility, even if it requires making some sacrifice to do so. Parents have the responsibility of promoting the development of their children, and even if a child has been irresponsible, it is important to go the extra mile in supporting autonomy and promoting development. In the case of the baby-sitter, however, with whom the woman had only a superficial, business relationship, she did not have a responsibility to promote his development. Not asking him back would be administering consequences, but there is no necessity for her to go further—unless, of course, she wants to. Had he been an actual employee of hers, someone who worked for her full-time, she would appropriately have taken somewhat greater responsibility, but he was not.

Part of the reason it is easy to confuse autonomy support and permissiveness is that people find it hard to admit that they are being permissive, so they misportray their permissive behavior as autonomy support. I remember one evening a couple of years ago when I looked after my violin-playing friend Lisa. I guess she must have been about four at the time. As the evening wore on, she became increasingly overstimulated, and when it was time for the usual routine—brushing teeth, story, and bed—she was quite hyperactive. There I was, someone who thinks about limit-setting a lot, and yet I found it hard to do what I knew to be the right thing—I found it hard to set limits with Lisa. The experience was an unsettling one for me, and as I probed my own reluctance to step up to the situation, the truth became perfectly clear, though not so easy to admit. I was reluctant to set limits—even autonomy-supportive limits—because I somehow feared that Lisa would like me less. Out of my own need to be loved by a four-year-old, I was shirking my responsibility as a caregiver.

W e are at a time in history when many parents are overworked as they try to accomplish the near impossible of balancing home and career. And because of this, there is a tendency among many parents, who really don't have as much time for their children as they would like, to feel guilty about it and to be permissive with their children as a way of appeasing their own guilt. It is a very similar dynamic to the problem I faced with Lisa.

Some overworked parents respond to the stress by being more demanding and critical of their children rather than permissive. In the worst cases, these parents essentially act out their aggression against their children. When their children don't respond as they'd like, when their children push them to the limit, they get angry and lash out. I've seen it many times, in the aisles of my local supermarket and the booths of my local family restaurant. Parents feel pressures from their own agendas, and if their children interfere with an agenda, they get agitated and end up yelling at the children, or shaking them.

Any child can push parents to their limits, especially when they are low on inner resources. When they are tired, stressed at work, or burdened by unfinished business, it is easy either to be permissive, or alternatively to become demanding, critical, and abusive when the child—or student or employee—is not acting as they would like. Everyone is vulnerable to this, but the important thing is that people not delude themselves into thinking they are being autonomy supportive when they are actually being permissive, and that they not delude themselves into thinking they are setting limits when they are actually aggressing.

People are entitled to their tensions and conflicts, but if they recognize these frustrations for what they are, if they own up to them, their children (or students or employees) will be less likely to pay the costs for the frustrations. By being aware of their own internal pressures and conflicts, people in one-up positions will be more able to facilitate effective accommodations between the individuals they teach, care for, or supervise, and the society that beckons.

EIGHT

The Self in a Social World

One of the things that has amazed me about the hundreds of bright, accomplished college students I've known through the years is how many of them have told me they don't express their real feelings and beliefs. If they did, they say, they would feel selfish or guilty, and people wouldn't like them. They can't be who they really are because of fear or shame.

These students hold introjects about who and what they should be, and those introjects are firmly anchored in their psyches. Some students even say they have no real sense of themselves separate from all the shoulds, musts, and have-to's. Overpowered by these introjects, the young people present a facade—a kind of false self—for they have lost touch with their true self. They have found acceptance from others by taking on an alien identity, by rigidly introjecting, rather than flexibly integrating, aspects of their social world.

I remember the case of a young man, Arthur, who had a very active mind. As a boy, he tended to question the nature of the world and to form coherent opinions. But this kind of behavior was anathema to the rigid family that raised him. When, at the age of nine, he wondered out loud about the purpose of life, his mother responded, "We don't ask questions like that." When, a year or so later, he thoughtfully criticized one of his father's favorite writers, his father responded, "Who are you to feel so superior to this great man?" In each case, his parents doused his inquisitive nature and he had to learn not to think out loud. Indeed, he seemed to lose all interest in abstract thoughts and big ideas.

The story of his home life is not an unusual one; many students have told me similar ones, although this one had a happier ending than most. Arthur was extremely intelligent, and when he reached college and found support for independent thought, his inquisitiveness was gradually rekindled. Eventually it flourished. But in the more common scenario, students who have been subjected to such controlling family environments, report an inability or an unwillingness to find their inner strengths and desires. They are anxious and fearful that something awful will happen if they make contact with the self that is within them.

One former student, Barbara, wrote that she always tries to satisfy others, that she does whatever they want. She went on to say that this is fine with her, so nothing is lost. I knew Barbara quite well when she wrote those lines, and I couldn't help but think that her doing what others want was not something she really chose, not something that really was fine with her. Instead, it seemed to me, she felt compelled to go along with what others wanted because she was terrified of the consequences if she did not.

In the worst cases, students can't even verbalize that they are being controlled by introjects and by others' demands. They don't have as much insight as Barbara had, and they don't even realize they are suppressing their inner self. I have to infer it from their ongoing display of anxious, rigid behavior patterns and their insistence about what they *have* to do. These students have actually lost touch with a true self. Having fully accepted the introjects in a desperate attempt for approval, they are left with nothing that truly feels like them, and they can't even acknowledge that. The potentials of their intrinsic self have gotten lost; a mature, true self has never developed; and they can't even face up to it.

One of the risks associated with being part of a unit—a family group, say, or society—is that people may be forced to give up or hide who they really are. They may feel obliged to relinquish their autonomy and true self in order to fit in. Integration, which represents optimal development and is in the best interests of both the children and their socializing agents, requires supports for both autonomy and relatedness, yet all too often socializing agents work against themselves, by attempting to control with contingent love, when autonomy support is what's needed. If autonomy is pitted against relatedness its toll can be a person's self.

M ost modern psychologists and sociologists view the self as socially programmed, which means that people's concepts of themselves are said to develop as the social world defines them. According to that view, when others praise you for being friendly, you come to see yourself as a friendly person. When others worry about whether you will succeed, you develop a sense of doubt about your abilities. When others interrupt your activities to show you how to do them better, you accept the belief that you are not very competent. For these theorists, whatever the social world programs us to be, that is what constitutes our self.

The problem with that view of the self as socially defined is that it makes no distinction between a true and false self. It fails to recognize that we each begin with an intrinsic self (nascent though it be), as well as the capacities to continuously elaborate and refine that self. Thus, self can develop in accord with its nature, or it can be programmed by society. But the self that results from these two processes will be very different.

The intrinsic self is not a genetically programmed entity that simply unfolds with time, however. It is instead a set of potentials, interests, and capabilities that interact with the world, each affecting the other. At any given time, self is the developmental outcome of this dialectical relationship. When the process operates effectively, true self is the result; when the process goes awry, the result is a less-true self. As such, the development of self is significantly influenced by the social world, but the self is not constructed by that world. Instead, individuals play an active role in the development of self, and true self develops as the social world supports the individual's activity.

True self begins with the intrinsic self—with our inherent interests and potentials and our organismic tendency to integrate new aspects of our experience. As true self is elaborated and refined, people develop an ever greater sense of responsibility. Out of their needs for autonomy, competence, and relatedness, people develop a willingness to give to others, to respond with what is needed. By integrating such values and behaviors, people become more responsible, while at the same time retaining their sense of personal freedom.

But integration and development of true self require that people's intrinsic needs be satisfied. When the social world within which people develop is autonomy supportive—when it provides optimal challenges and the opportunity for choice and self-initiation—true self will flourish. When the social world accepts people for who they are, providing love as they explore their inner and outer environments, true self will develop optimally. But when these needs are not satisfied, the process will be thwarted. The development of true self requires autonomy support—it requires noncontingent acceptance and love.

One of the most common approaches to discipline in modern society involves making the provision of love, acceptance, and esteem contingent upon people's behaving in certain ways. This withdrawal-of-love approach underlies one of the tragic aspects of life, namely that in many circumstances autonomy and relatedness are turned against each other by people in one-up positions. This does not mean that the needs are by nature antagonistic, only that the social world can capitalize on people's vulnerability to being controlled—to having their autonomy robbed—by their need to be related to others. The practice of making love contingent is one of the more controlling ways we can treat children (as well as peers), because it forces them to relinquish autonomy to retain love, or alternatively, to "live as an island."

Research has repeatedly confirmed that controlling contexts impair development by stifling integration and promoting introjection. The contingent administration of love thus represents yet another instance of people—most notably parents—working against themselves. By being invested in getting children to behave properly, parents use withdrawal of love, and in the process not only hinder internalization of regulations, but more importantly, hinder development of true self.

Children's accepting the values, regulatory processes, and conceptions of themselves that are offered to them by the social world is natural, but when the world's offerings are accompanied by control—when receiving love is dependent on accepting the world's values and regulations—children will, at best, only introject them, swallowing them whole rather than integrating them into their developing self.

Introjected material is not part of the integrated or true self, but instead endures as rigid demands, concepts, and evaluations that are the basis of a false self. Alice Miller, in *The Drama of the Gifted Child,* explained that false self develops as children accept the identity that controlling caretakers want them to have. In an attempt to please their parents and gain contingent love, children gradually intuit what it is that their parents want—what it is that they, the children, hope will gain them the love and avoid the reproach of their controlling parents.

Introjects can be powerful motivators, relentlessly pushing people to think, feel, or behave in particular ways. But they also have a variety of side effects that attest to their maladaptation. Introjection is strongly related to anxiety—people live in fear of failure and loss of esteem. It is also accompanied by an inner conflict that rages between what we metaphorically think of as the internalized controller who demands, cajoles, and evaluates and the person within the same skin who is being directed and criticized. Introjection is the process that facilitates the emergence of a false self—the emergence of a set of rigid rules and identities—and it is a process through which people can lose contact with who they really are.

Once, when I was doing therapy with a man in his early twen-

ties—tall and conservatively dressed in double-knit trousers and a
bland tie—I became increasingly aware of how inexpressive he was,
how robotlike, how tired. As the therapy evolved toward a discussion of the young man's authoritarian father, I noticed an expression
of feeling in just one small part of his body: a clenched right fist. I
invited him to hit the clenched fist into the palm of his other hand,
which he did. Instantly, his whole body went startlingly rigid, his
face contorted. The very notion that he might be striking back at his
father, even symbolically, was so unsettling that the young man was
virtually paralyzed. The false sense of being that took the form of
what his father thought he should be was incredibly powerful and
hard to fight against.

The panic and rigidity slowly passed, and within an hour he was
back in more or less the same shape he had been before the episode
occurred. His introjects were intact, and it was almost as if the incident had not occurred. Indeed, the young man found it hard even to
discuss the incident during subsequent meetings, because having
angry thoughts about his father left him feeling like a terrible person.
Still, he had gotten a glimpse of what his problem was, and continuing therapy did help him deal with the rage he felt for his father. It
even helped him regain some of his innate vitality. But it was a tough
road. Caught in a coercive vise, the man had lost a true sense of self,
and with it had gone his intrinsic motivation for life—the curiosity,
the striving, the boldness that could energize his everyday experience. Fortunately, a lot of hard work allowed him to recapture a
little of it.

The use of contingent love and esteem as a means of control not
only promotes introjection, but it has the even sorrier consequence of teaching people to esteem *themselves* contingently. Just as
they once had to live up to external demands to gain love and esteem
from others, they now have to live up to introjects to gain love and
esteem from themselves. They feel like worthy people only if they do
as the introjects demand. When my client was angry with his father,

he felt like an unworthy person, and that contingent feeling of self-worth gave enormous power to the introjects. Indeed, it gave them so much power that they virtually paralyzed him when he briefly dared to stand up to them.

Ego involvement is a term that psychologists use to refer to the process of people's feelings of worth being dependent upon specified outcomes. When people hold introjects and those introjects are buttressed by contingent worth, the people are said to be ego-involved. A man is ego-involved in his work if his feelings of worth are dependent on amassing a fortune from the work, and a woman is ego-involved in her exercise if her feelings of worth are dependent on winning a competition at her health club.

Ryan and his colleagues have done several studies exploring the effects of ego involvement. In a typical experiment, one group of subjects would be ego-involved or motivated by a threat to the self while another group would be task-involved or motivated by the interest and value of the activity itself. Results of the studies consistently showed that ego involvement undermined intrinsic motivation for the task and led subjects to report more pressure, tension, and anxiety about performance.

Ego involvement develops when people are contingently esteemed by others, so it goes hand in hand with introjection of values and regulations. When self-esteem is hinged on performance outcomes, people struggle to maintain a facade. They pressure themselves to appear a certain way to others so they will feel good about themselves. This, of course, detracts from interest and enthusiasm. Indeed, it bolsters a false self while continuing to undermine development of true self.

When ego-involved, people focus on how they look to others, so they are forever judging how they stack up. A girl who is ego-involved in her grades, for example, will forever be checking to see how others did on a test so she will know whether she did "well enough."

Research has shown that ego involvement not only undermines intrinsic motivation, but as one would expect, it impairs learning and creativity, and it tends to diminish performance on any task where flexible thinking and problem solving are required. The rigidities of ego involvement interfere with effective information processing; they lead people to be shallower, more superficial, in how they think about problems.

In short, ego involvement is constructed on a tenuous sense of self, and it works against being autonomous. To become more autonomous—more self-determined—thus requires that people detach from their ego involvements, that they gradually give them up.

Mel Wearing, a slugger for the Rochester Red Wings, is a powerful guy and a hotshot hitter. When he first started on the team, people were expecting him to hit a home run every time he stepped to the plate. The problem was that he was also expecting it of himself. According to his own account, when he joined the Red Wings he set out to impress people—to knock it out of the park time after time. He gripped the bat too tightly and swung too hard, he said. At the beginning of each season he would think to himself, "This is going to be my year," and he would bear down on himself. He tried to use his power to do the job, but it didn't work. His performance was disappointing, and he felt bad about himself.

Finally, one year, he realized that he would be better off if he stopped worrying about it, if he stopped trying so hard, if he stopped hinging his self-worth on being a slugger. All he had to do, he said to himself, was make contact with the ball. And sure enough, the less hard he tried, the better he did. He began living up to his potential because he stopped trying to. He had given up his ego involvement. It's a paradox, but it's true.

Charlotte Selver developed the practice of Sensory Awareness. It is an approach to allowing one's inner functioning, to coming more into contact with who one really is. She's had many notable students—people like psychiatrists Erich Fromm, Fritz Perls, and Clara Thompson, for example—who have worked with her to develop a deeper sense of inner peace and a greater sensitivity to their surroundings. I once heard Charlotte make the comment, "If you dare to be fat, then you can be thin." Such a simple way to say something so profound.

She was highlighting the power struggle that exists for so many people between the ego involvements that pressure them to be thin and the part of themselves that resists being pressured. By trying to force themselves to lose weight with the threat that they will hate themselves if they don't, people create resistance. They undermine themselves by pressuring themselves and then resisting the pressure. Out of spite for the introjected controls they sabotage themselves. To lose weight—or to change any other behavior for that matter—people will be more successful if they start by giving up the ego involvement, if they start by getting themselves out of the power struggle with their introjects and out of the self-hatred that inevitably follows. When they do that, "then they can be thin."

Think of it in terms of the master and slave. The master in your head thinks you should be thin and hates you for being fat. So the master criticizes and threatens, cajoles and humiliates. And, not surprisingly, although a part of you tries to please the master, another part of you wants to defy, to get back at the master. That of course is easy enough to do: Just stay fat. The problem is that the master is you too, so spiting the master is spiting yourself.

Allow yourself to fail and you will be more likely to succeed. That's what Charlotte Selver was saying, and that's what Mel Wearing finally realized.

R ecognizing how introjects and ego involvements motivate through a process of contingent self-worth points to the very important fact that there are really two types of self-esteem. We refer to them as true self-esteem and contingent self-esteem. True self-esteem represents a sound, stable sense of oneself, built on a solid foundation of believing in one's worth as a human being. It accompanies a well-developed true self in which intrinsic motivation has been maintained, extrinsic limits and regulations have been well integrated, and the processes necessary for regulating one's emotions have been developed. True self-esteem thus accompanies freedom and responsibility.

True self-esteem is not, however, the same thing as thinking you can do no wrong. People with true self-esteem have a sense of whether behaviors are right or wrong because true self-esteem is accompanied by integrated values and regulations. Such individuals evaluate their behaviors, but their feelings of worth as people are not riding on those evaluations.

There is another type of self-esteem, however, that is less stable, less securely based in a fundamental sense of worth. It is present under some conditions but vanishes under others, leaving people depleted and self-derogatory. This is contingent self-esteem. When people are pressured and controlled to achieve particular outcomes, their self-esteem is often dependent on how those things turn out. Indeed, ego involvements gain power over people because they are accompanied by contingent self-esteem. If a man's self-esteem rides on continually closing big business deals—especially ones that are bigger than his colleagues'—and if he were continually quite successful, he would generally feel pretty good about himself. But those feelings would be more ephemeral than real. They would likely take the form of self-aggrandizement—of a big ego, so to speak—rather than a solid sense of self, and they would tend to be formulated in terms of being better than others rather than simply being good and worthy like others.

People with true self-esteem are able to esteem others and accept others' frailties rather than evaluating and deprecating them. I once heard Elie Wiesel, winner of the Nobel Peace Prize, say, "I am here as a witness to describe, not as a judge to evaluate." Of course, much of what he has described in his writings about the Holocaust is morally repugnant, and he surely deplores it, but his comment was focused on human potential, on what is good and possible for each of us. He went on to say, "I have hope because there is no other possibility for life." These are the kinds of words that would be spoken by someone with true self-esteem.

Countless popular books have extolled the importance of high self-esteem, but their failure to distinguish between true self-esteem and contingent self-esteem has led to questionable prescriptions. Authors advise parents, teachers, and friends to praise others—to remind them what good people they are. Of course, conveying to others your belief in their worthiness is noble, but praising does not necessarily do that. Indeed, it may have just the opposite effect if it is delivered contingently.

Carl Rogers advocated what he called noncontingent positive regard. In essence, he was suggesting that regard from others (and, most importantly, from ourselves) is our inalienable right. We are worthy by virtue of the fact that we are alive. Praise is usually different. It is typically made contingent on getting an A on an exam, eating all those vegetables, or cleaning your room. Its hidden message is that you would not be worthy if you had not hit the target.

Praise runs the risk of bolstering contingent self-esteem rather than true self-esteem, and in the process it strengthens a controlling dynamic in which people become dependent on the praise. They then behave to get more praise so they will feel worthy—even if only for a moment. And in so doing, they further erode their autonomy.

The most important relationship in many people's lives is one particular peer relationship, usually with a romantic partner but sometimes with a best friend. That person is someone to turn to, someone to count on, someone to support you. That person is someone who will listen, who will understand when no one else seems to. But that person is also someone to give to, to provide for, to hear, and to understand. The most important relationship in many people's lives is one of mutual dependence. It is one that allows them to satisfy their need for relatedness by being dependent on others who are also dependent on them.

Such relationships are essential, and many people structure their lives around them. But in considering a mutually dependent relationship there is the important question of whether in the midst of the mutual dependence there is also mutual autonomy—and mutual autonomy support. With people who love each other, autonomy support is a two-way street.

What characterizes the most mature and satisfying relationships is that the true self of one person relates to the true self of another. Each is dependent on the other, but each maintains his or her autonomy, his or her integrity, his or her sense of self. To the extent that each is in the relationship autonomously, with a true sense of choice, the relationship will be healthy, and each partner will be able to respond from his or her true self and will be able to support the individuality and idiosyncracies of the other.

Psychologists Marc Blais, Robert Vallerand, and their colleagues at the University of Quebec in Montreal did a study to explore people's reasons for participating in their current romantic relationship. They adapted the Self-Regulation Questionnaire developed by Ryan and Connell to assess the extent to which people's motivation for staying in the relationship was autonomous—the extent to which they were there with a true sense of choice and personal desire rather than feeling some pressure or control for being there. The researchers found that the autonomy of each partner was essential for the couple's relational happiness. Those individuals who were autonomous in relating to their partner expressed the highest level of satisfaction in their relationship. Many of the people who were studied, however, were not autonomous, but instead felt quite controlled. These people did not feel free in the relationship. They related to their partner out of obligation. In these relationships the true selves of the partners were not engaged.

I once had a therapy client who phoned my office for an initial visit and said her name was Mrs. Cutlass. When she arrived for the visit she introduced herself to me as Mrs. Cutlass, and every succeeding time she identified herself—on the phone or in person—it was as Mrs. Cutlass. She made the appointment because she had hit her husband with a piece of firewood, and the event had shaken her badly. (I suspect he had been a bit shaken, too.) She said that on and off for the last few weeks she had found herself angry at him, for no particular reason. This anger was very unsettling for her. In all their twenty-eight years of marriage she had never felt this way before.

She had married right out of college and started a family within a couple of years. She was a model housewife and mother. She attended unwaveringly to the needs of her husband, always putting them ahead of her own. She was similarly attentive to the desires of her three children, the youngest of whom had just graduated from college. She drove them to football practice and music lessons, she was a Scout leader, and she helped out with various school and church events.

I am sure her friends thought she loved her husband very much, that she was a devoted and loving wife. And in a sense she was. But it was an imbalanced love. She supported her husband in all his endeavors, giving him whatever he wanted. On those occasions in therapy when I asked her what she wanted for herself from the relationship, or from life more generally, she could think of nothing to say. She wanted to be a good wife and mother, to be sure, and she wanted to be thought well of for how she had performed those roles, but there seemed to be nothing she wanted for herself.

She was able to acknowledge that there seemed to be a large gap in her life now that her children no longer needed her, but she could not identify any aspirations. She did not articulate any short-term desires, like having some time to herself to try painting, or having her husband take more interest in her feelings. Nor could she specify any longer-term desires, like starting a career, or finding something else to devote herself to.

I thought it was very telling that she had introduced herself to me as Mrs. Cutlass. She is the only client I can ever recall who introduced herself without using her first name as well as her last. It was as if she had no identity of her own.

Mrs. Cutlass was the wife of Mr. Cutlass, and of course the mother of his children. She was Mrs. Cutlass in a one-down sense, and for twenty-eight years she had thought that was enough. But something seemed to be happening. Just being Mrs. Cutlass was no longer enough, although it took her several months to realize that and to accept that her hitting her husband had something to do with this issue. The anger, which took twenty-eight years to surface, stemmed from her identity's having been subsumed by his.

Ultimately, of course, it was she who was responsible for the subjugation of her self, even though her husband obviously contributed. And this realization was the starting point for figuring out what she wanted for herself, and how she could get it. As she became more aware of her own wants, needs, and feelings, she was in a position to choose how to express and satisfy them. Gradually, she worked to change her relationship with her husband by identifying what she wanted in the relationship and negotiating to get it.

Mature relationships are characterized by two individuals' interacting openly with each other, unencumbered by ego involvements, introjected evaluations, or self-deprecations. In mature, mutual relationships, the one-up, one-down aspect that characterizes so many other relationships in life is not only absent in the structural sense but is absent in actuality. Each person is autonomous, and each supports the autonomy of the other.

In such relationships, each partner is able to give to the other, expecting nothing in return and creating no obligations for the other. The giving comes from the true self, and thus the person experiences *wanting* to give. It is not a giving like that of Mrs. Cutlass, for hers came from an introjected set of beliefs about how she should behave as a wife and mother, rather than from an integrated self. Although she was a loving wife and mother, who did much good for others, her giving was at the cost of a solid sense of her self.

When two people are relating maturely, each will be able to ask the other for what he or she wants or needs, fully trusting that the other will say "no" if he or she does not want to give it. Just as giving sets up no expectations and receiving creates no obligations, in optimal relationships asking for something from one's partner carries no expectations of receiving it and creates no obligation for the partner to give it. In these mature relationships, people freely give and they freely withhold giving. There is a balancing of getting what one needs for oneself and giving to the other. Giving is not at the expense of one's self but instead is wholly endorsed by the self.

In such relationships, each partner can express his or her feelings freely and each can hear the other's feelings without defensiveness. When, for example, a man says to his partner, "I am angry at you," he will realize it does not necessarily mean his partner did something wrong. Rather, it means that he did not get what he wanted. Being aware of feelings is important for the development and functioning of the true self, and communicating them is important for intimacy in relationships. But when people "own them," when people understand that their feelings are caused by the relation of events to their own wants, needs, and expectations, they will be able to express the feelings constructively, without engaging in aggression. It also allows people to think about how to get what they want or need without necessarily requiring that their partners change.

It is not easy for another to listen to one's anger without becoming defensive, but the more able one is to own the anger, the more likely it is that the other will be able to hear it. By owning feelings and sharing them with another, two people become ever closer.

Erich Fromm, in his enormously popular book *The Art of Loving,* pointed out that loving someone is very hard work. The thing that is hard about loving is freeing yourself from the introjects, the rigidities, the blaming, and the self-derogation that interfere with being able to relate honestly from your true self. What is hard is being psychologically free enough to make genuine contact.

NINE

When Society Corrupts

I t's just half a century since the Second World War was won, and
people began to sleep easier with the American Dream dancing
in their heads. Prosperity lay ahead for all, and people were con-
fident that hard work would bring them the leisure and luxury of
their dream. After all, ours is a society that favors self-reliance. People who own the tools of production and use them effectively ac-
cumulate wealth, and those without the advantage of ownership can
nonetheless be comfortable if they work hard and submit to the authority of the owners.

The American Dream was a motivating force for many people,
and acceptance of what Charles Reich called the generalized authority of believing there are certain ways that things "should be done"
was the means to obtain the dream. So people knuckled down to a
wholesome life of hard work. Unfortunately, the dream has not
materialized for most people. At least not in the form they dreamed
it. People work more now than in 1950—nearly an hour a day more,
on average. Dual-income families have become the norm, so with no
one home during the day, non-work time is usually gobbled up by
kids and chores. There is little time left for leisure, and luxury has not
materialized. Many families have two cars, a cleaning lady, a phone
machine, and a VCR, but far from feeling like luxuries, these have
become necessities for coping with the stresses of an overextended
life.

Still, except during that brief period called the sixties, most people have bought into the American Dream, continuing to hope that one day the beautiful life—the life of Julia Roberts, Michael Jordan, or Barbra Streisand, say—might be theirs. And even if that glamour does not come to pass, a strong dedication to work may at least bring people an RV or Florida condo, along with the possibility of sending their children to a good college.

I remember a man from a therapy group years ago, a highly successful business executive I'll call Kevin Jacobs. An articulate and well-groomed man in his mid-forties, he was a satisfied husband and father of three teenagers. The family had an attractive urban life, with the children in private schools, and there was every indication that they had achieved a modest version of the American Dream. Kevin entered therapy because he had not been sleeping well for the past few months, and he felt an unpleasant constriction in his chest. A series of visits to his physician and a number of medical tests revealed no medical problems, but the uneasiness remained.

Therapy started slowly for Kevin as he spoke about how well everything was going for him. But then at one point, when he was talking about his son—the middle child—he went pale. His eyes watered, and he found it hard to talk. It was almost as if an acute depression had overtaken him in an instant. His anxiety was intense, but gradually he was able to talk about the flood of thoughts that had begun in that fateful incident. As he did, the anxiety dissipated, and he began to plan meaningful changes in his life.

The memory that triggered all this was of his son, at age six, a private-school first-grader who had a part in a school play. The son was excited, and the family looked forward to the Friday evening event. But on that Friday evening, at the time his son was on stage, Kevin was changing planes at O'Hare Airport, returning home from a business meeting. The memory was of the son's disappointment when Kevin told him he would have to miss the play.

The event is common enough these days, when so much of our work takes us out of town or ties us up in the evening. As a single event, it was surely not of such great significance for Kevin or for his son. But it was not just a single event. It was a symbol of how, for twenty years, Kevin's career had come first. For twenty years he had put in sixty- to seventy-hour weeks, all in order to be a good provider, to give his family the American Dream. Suddenly, it had occurred to him (as it has to many other fathers in similar moments of great sadness) that in the process he had not really been part of the family. His children were teenagers and he hadn't watched them grow up.

In the succeeding months, Kevin made some changes. He reordered his priorities. He shortened his work week, and he concentrated on deepening his relationships with his wife and children. It was not all smooth, but it was a kind of happy ending. He did not have to go through a divorce or some other traumatic event—as so many others do—before he discovered what was really important to him.

And what was it that was different now? He was able to achieve a balance in the satisfaction of his basic needs. He had always felt quite effective in his career, so the need for competence had been well satisfied. But now his relationships were deeper, so he experienced a fuller satisfaction of his need for relatedness. Furthermore, in all realms of his life, he felt more autonomous, more like he was truly making his own choices. He was no longer *driven* by his work.

Surely the American Dream, with its emphasis on materialism, is a potent motivator. It kept Kevin chained to his desk for twenty years. And it allowed his children to keep up with the changing fashions in athletic shoes. But it cost Kevin and his family dearly in terms of personal satisfaction. Just how common this phenomenon is—just how pervasive the negative consequences of the American Dream are—is an interesting question.

The concept of materialism has been widely discussed and hotly debated. On the one hand, politicians and economists call for more spending to boost the GNP, while on the other hand critics and psychologists such as Paul Wachtel argue that affluence impoverishes the soul. Only recently has psychological data begun to shed light on this controversy. Richard Ryan and former graduate student Tim

Kasser have collected relevant data from hundreds of subjects—college students and adults who span the spectrum of age as well as social and economic status.

The researchers focused on six types of life aspirations. Three were what we call extrinsic aspirations—the stuff the American Dream is made of. They were the aspirations for being wealthy, famous, and physically attractive. They were the ones where the desired outcomes are instrumental for still other ends. Money brings power and material possessions. Fame opens doors and may lead to a shower of gifts. A beautiful image provides options for glamorous escorts, marketing opportunities, and unending attention.

In contrast, the other three aspirations were referred to as intrinsic because they provide their own reward and help to satisfy people's innate needs for competence, autonomy, and relatedness. These three were: having satisfying personal relationships, making contributions to the community, and growing as individuals. Of course, it is possible that a satisfying personal relationship with an influential person could open doors, and that making community contributions could bring acclaim, so there could be some instrumental advantages to the intrinsic aspirations. But the intrinsic aspirations are really quite different from the extrinsic ones; they are satisfying in their own right. People feel significant personal gratification from the three intrinsic outcomes whether or not they lead to other ends.

All of the six aspirations are ones that most of us hold, and even the extrinsic aspiration for financial success is important—at least to some degree—for living a satisfying life. It is undeniably reasonable to want to own a small piece of the earth on which to have a dwelling, and to strive for food, medical care, and some aesthetic pleasure for yourself and your family. But what the researchers were primarily interested in is what happens when people's desire for one or more of these life goals is out of balance with the others.

In the research, individuals rated the importance to themselves of each of these life aspirations. Using a sophisticated statistical procedure, Kasser and Ryan indexed the degree to which individuals' cravings for one of the goals was out of balance with the others. For example, if Kevin Jacobs had completed the questionnaire before therapy, his craving for material success would undoubtedly have been out of balance with his aspiration for community contributions and personal relationships.

The researchers found that if any of the three extrinsic aspirations—for money, fame, or beauty—was very high for an individual relative to the three intrinsic aspirations, the individual was also more likely to display poorer mental health. For example, having an unusually strong aspiration for material success was associated with narcissism, anxiety, depression, and poorer social functioning as rated by a trained clinical psychologist. The other extrinsic aspirations were similarly associated with indicators of poorer psychological functioning. In contrast, strong aspirations for any of the intrinsic goals—meaningful relationships, personal growth, and community contributions—were positively associated with well-being. People who strongly desired to contribute to their community, for example, had more vitality and higher self-esteem. When people organize their behavior in terms of intrinsic strivings (relative to extrinsic strivings) they seem more content—they feel better about who they are and display more evidence of psychological health.

Part of the difficulty posed by extrinsic aspirations such as wealth and fame is that people fear they will never be able to achieve them, and some psychologists have suggested that these negative expectancies are what cause ill-being. If people place very strong importance on achieving any goal and believe they won't be able to attain the goal, they will feel unhappy and perhaps depressed. I once knew a young playwright who had worked hard for two or three years writing a play about the stresses and confusions of family life. The play was substantially autobiographical, and he had had enough positive feedback about it from writers and theater people that he held high expectations for success in regional theater and then on the Great White Way. It was remarkable how closely his moods and general demeanor were tied to developments with the play. When something positive happened, he was ebullient and dreaming of a dazzling opening night, but when he encountered an obstacle his expectations plummeted and he became depressed. With his strongly held goal, his negative beliefs about the likelihood of achieving the goal predicted his dysphoria.

Kasser and Ryan, in their research on life aspirations, asked respondents to report their beliefs about how likely it was that they would achieve each of the three extrinsic goals and each of the three intrinsic goals. Recall that the first finding indicated that if people held extrinsic goals very dear, they had tenuous mental health. The second important finding was that, *even if* the respondents thought the chances of achieving the dearly held extrinsic goals were excellent, they still displayed poor mental health. Holding extrinsic aspirations and believing they won't be able to achieve them will surely leave people dyspeptic, but the less obvious and more penetrating finding from this research is that holding very strong extrinsic aspirations and believing strongly that they *will* be able to achieve them was also associated with poorer psychological health. It is more the type of aspirations people hold very strongly than the expectations they have about achieving them that is the critical predictor of well-being.

These studies brought a whole new dimension to the research on personal autonomy. Whereas earlier studies had focused on issues like the quality of one's performance and experience, these studies drew direct linkages between types of motivation and individuals' mental health. It seems that people who are the healthiest focus on developing satisfying personal relationships, growing as individuals, and contributing to their community. Surely, they also aspire to sufficient financial success to live comfortably. But wealth, fame, and beauty do not disproportionately occupy the consciousnesses of these people the way they dominate the experiences of individuals who are less psychologically stable.

Underlying a strong emphasis on extrinsic strivings is a tenuous hold on one's self. Those extrinsic goals bring attention to what one has rather than who one is. They constitute a facade, a socially derived persona that lacks a solid grounding. In the absence of feeling deeply satisfied, of achieving gratification of one's intrinsic needs, people come to desire the more superficial goals.

Unduly strong extrinsic aspirations can thus be understood as representing aspects of a false self. They have potence because people's contingent self-esteem is dependent upon the attainment of these goals. When people have been continually subjected to contingent love and esteem, particularly when they were young, they learn to look to external criteria as the basis for judging their worth—initially the things their parents indicated were necessary, and subsequently what society implicitly or explicitly advocated. In developing an orientation toward external criteria for judging one's worth, people become particularly vulnerable to the forces of society. They are more likely to adopt the values that society seems to endorse. Most notably, they will adopt the values that are inherent in advertising—values like accumulating more and fancier possessions, and values for which the criteria are readily apparent, like wealth, fame, or looks. Extrinsic aspirations, of course, fit exactly this description.

K asser, Ryan, and colleagues investigated the developmental antecedents of the different types of aspirations with the hope of shedding further light on the dynamic relationship between aspirations and mental health. To do this, they used data collected from mothers and their children over a fourteen-year period. In line with their speculations, the researchers found that eighteen-year-olds who placed undue weight on extrinsic aspirations such as wealth had mothers who had been controlling (rather than autonomy supportive) and cold (rather than nurturing) when the children were young. In contrast, mothers who had been warm, involved, and autonomy supportive had children who grew up to desire more intrinsic life outcomes.

The research on aspirations added greatly to the emerging picture, for it confirmed that failing to be autonomy supportive and involved with your children can promote a more extrinsic orientation, as well as more introjection and a more contingent sense of self. This extrinsic orientation and the concomitant sense of contingent worth results from the children's not being able to satisfy their fundamental intrinsic needs for autonomy, competence, and relatedness, and it is accordingly linked to poorer mental health. When individuals are strongly extrinsically oriented, they lack a firm foundation for well-being.

The term human needs is commonly used and typically equated with the idea of a want or a desire. What a person would like to have is often said to be what he or she needs. But that is an imprecise and misleading use of the concept of human need. Instead, in line with Abraham Maslow, we define a human need as an organismic condition—whether physiological or psychological—that must be ongoingly satisfied for people to remain healthy and that will result in dysfunction if it is not. Ryan and Kasser's research provides clear support for this view and helps to verify that competence, autonomy, and relatedness are indeed fundamental human needs. In contrast, however, what are often called needs for money and fame, say, are not needs at all. They may be wants or desires, and they may be extremely potent organizers of one's life activities, but they are not basic psychological needs.

For a society to function effectively, its individual members must, to some extent, adopt the society's values and mores. But internalizing values and the willingness to live by them is a delicate matter on two grounds. First, to be effective as an individual, a person's values and the accompanying motivation to behave must be integrated—they must become part of a coherent self. If they do not, they will subjugate the self to society. And, second, if the values and mores that society offers to individuals—values like extreme materialism—are out of kilter with the individuals' fundamental human needs, the internalization process can go awry. People may internalize the values, but they will pay a serious cost as they continually strive to live up to those unusually strong extrinsic values.

Holding extrinsic values that are substantially more salient than intrinsic values is evidence of a lack of integration of these values. If people's valuing of money were integrated into their sense of self, that aspiration would be in balance with the others—it would be valued for its utility in allowing them to live a full and balanced life, providing meaningful opportunities for relatedness, offering aesthetic experiences, helping others, and supporting public institutions. If their aspirations for money were well integrated, they would, for example, be willing to make contributions to their public radio station, or the Boy Scouts, without needing to be acknowledged or applauded. They would contribute to these, or whatever other public organization fits their individual taste, because of their sense of general connectedness to others and their feeling of responsibility for the general good.

I am not suggesting that people should make their contributions anonymously. The point is that if the motivation were truly an intrinsic desire to contribute to the community, and if their regard for money were well integrated with their intrinsic aspirations and with other aspects of themselves, they would be willing to contribute anonymously. The contribution would be its own reward, and any acknowledgment would simply be a nice bonus.

The integration of extrinsic values—that is, the balance between them and intrinsic values—is to a considerable extent influenced by parenting styles, as the research by Kasser and Ryan indicated. Nurturing, autonomy-supportive parents are more likely to have children who have been able to integrate the extrinsic values. But all the blame does not lie at the feet of parents. Society, with the raging force of its emphasis on materialism, is a formidable obstacle to promoting a balance in the values of our children—and indeed of ourselves.

Money keeps people current, with flashy possessions, hot new gadgets, and coveted seats at sporting events and concerts. And, of course, it gives people power to stand out from the masses, to exercise their will over others, to look like someone special. So highly valued is money within our society that, according to James Pattern and Peter Kim in their book *The Day America Told the Truth,* about twenty-five percent of our citizens would be willing to abandon their entire family to receive ten million dollars; about seven percent would be willing to kill a stranger for that amount; and three percent would be willing to put their children up for adoption. Surrounded by such strongly held desires for money, the parenting task of promoting a balanced desire in our children for extrinsic and intrinsic goals is a daunting challenge.

One of the foundations of American society is individualism. Many of our heroes, both real and literary, have been independent individuals who have settled new territories or amassed enormous wealth. We hold a romantic view of the cowboys who roamed the west or the seamen who battled storms on the pages of our novels, and we have idolized the captains of industry after whom museums, libraries, and universities have been named.

Rags-to-riches stories abound in our cultural history and have been woven through countless textbooks to make the rather exaggerated point that "We can all make of ourselves whatever we'd like." This individualism for members of our society is a logical byproduct of the individualism of our society as a whole. It was evident in the Pilgrims, and it underlay the Revolutionary War. The new nation stood for self-governance, and it granted self-governance to its citizens. Individualism was proclaimed a societal value and both political and economic systems were developed to support that value.

As formally explicated by writer Ayn Rand and others, individualism holds to the primacy of individuals' rights. Each person's desires reign supreme and are their own justification. Whereas, according to Rand, altruism views individuals as a means to the ends of others, individualism views individuals as ends in their own right. From that perspective, it is thus a moral imperative that the beneficiary of an action be the person who acts, so individualism and selfishness are essentially equivalent. Both involve evaluating outcomes on the basis of self-interest. Interest of the whole—that is, of society—should not be a concern of the individual, they say. Instead, the good of society is theorized to result from all its citizens' pursuing their own individual interests. As such, public well-being is not considered a goal, but is assumed to be a corollary of individualism.

Like independence, individualism has also been confused with autonomy, and many writers have used the terms interchangeably. Yet the two concepts are profoundly different. The confusion stems from a superficial similarity in the definitions of the two concepts. Individualism refers to being free to pursue your own ends; it means that no external force (read: no government) will interfere with your attempts to get what you desire, so long as you do it legally. (The value of individualism also entails keeping laws to a minimum.) Similarly, autonomy can be defined as being volitional (i.e., free) in pursuing the goals that you choose. Both concepts thus have some relationship to freedom, and both convey the sense of self-rule. But the foci and meaning of the two concepts are very different.

Individualism is about self-interest, about acting to achieve and acquire for yourself. It encompasses being personally or emotionally independent (which was discussed in Chapter Six) but it goes far beyond independence to incorporate the sense of selfishness, of looking out just for yourself. Individualism stands in contrast to acting for the common good. The converse of individualism is collectivism. Here individuals' rights and goals are subordinated to the rights and goals of the whole. In a collective society, people are dependent on others, but their dependence is more than personal or emotional reliance; it is a structural interconnection in which all one's outcomes are intertwined with those of others. Family comes before individual; group comes before individual; society comes before individual. Individuals are expected to behave in ways that serve the common good rather than their own good. The well-being of individuals is thus viewed as a corollary of the strength of the collective, rather than the other way around.

Autonomy, in contrast, is about acting volitionally, with a sense of choice, flexibility, and personal freedom. It is about feeling a true willingness to behave responsibly, in accord with your interests and values. The converse of being autonomous is being controlled, which means that you are pressured to behave, think, or feel some particular way. Control is often exerted by others—by people in one-up positions, or by the society, but, of course, people can be controlling with themselves to satisfy their introjects. To pressure yourself, to force yourself to act, or to feel as if you have to do something is to undermine your own autonomy.

The hard-driving, competitive businessman who fights for more power and more wealth may be a rugged individualist, but he is not an exemplar of autonomy. To the extent that pursuit of his ends are pressured or coerced, even if from within, he is being individualistic but not autonomous. Many people, of course, find the notion of individualism very appealing, but its appeal comes more from their compulsion to achieve within the capitalist economic system than it does from their innate needs. Several writers such as psychologist Carol Gilligan have confused individualism and autonomy so their critiques have portrayed the concept of autonomy as a culprit when in fact what they were actually criticizing was masculine independence and Western individualism. To be autonomous in relating to others is hardly something that deserves critique.

Just as individualism can be controlled, so, too, can activity on behalf of the collective. The totalitarian communist regimes in Eastern Europe prior to 1989 were hideous examples of exactly that, with external, threatening contingencies as the instruments of control. Japan, though different and less oppressive than the Soviet Empire, also represents a version of controlled collectivism. In Japan, the group has traditionally come before the individual. It is a strong societal value, almost universally held within the culture. Family allegiance is understood to be mandatory and the honor of the family has even motivated suicides of family members who have lost face. Rather than being based in external coercion, however, Japan's means of control is an incredibly effective process of promoting the kind of internalization in which people take in values and use them rigidly on themselves. People control themselves in accord with the social mores of the culture, rather than being controlled by the agents of that culture.

Effective though it has been, however, there is increasing evidence that the fabric of the Japanese society is beginning to fray. Indictments for embezzlement and other collusion at high levels of the financial world attest to a growing sense of individualism, and social problems such as homelessness, while far less acute than in the U.S., are on the rise.

It is possible, and indeed quite common in U.S. society, to be individualistic in one's actions without being autonomous, just as it is possible to be collectivist without being autonomous, as has traditionally been the case in Japan.

Philosopher Robert Young, in providing a definition of autonomy much like ours, said that acting autonomously requires rational capacities and strength of will. Of course, individualism requires these as well. But autonomy, according to Young, also requires self-knowledge. This point is an extremely important one, for self-knowledge implies personality integration, and that is what distinguishes autonomy from individualism. Through self-knowledge one becomes more integrated and comes more into connection with one's true inner being—with one's intrinsic predilections and integrated values. Individualism, with its rational capacities and strength of will, can be autonomous only when accompanied by self-knowledge.

As noted earlier, self-knowledge (as opposed to self-deception) is a rather tricky concept. Self-knowledge begins with a relaxed attention to one's inner processes; it begins with genuine interest in oneself. What passes for self-knowledge is often not that at all, but instead involves an investment in seeing oneself, and being seen by others, in a particular way—as friendly, rich, intelligent, or whatever. When people are interested in their inner self in an honest way, they will be more able to give up ego involvements and be more eager to understand whatever they encounter in their inner exploration. Autonomy facilitates and is facilitated by this self-knowledge.

It is surely ironic that in our culture, which emphasizes individualism as a birthright, conformity is so evident. Although many Americans are no longer controlled by religious or community values, they are increasingly controlled by extrinsic outcomes, conforming with the symbols of status promulgated by the mass media. When you think about it, doesn't it seem rather silly that people wear labels on the outside of their clothing, rather than the inside?

Understanding that individualism often coexists with control rather than autonomy allows us to understand this seemingly paradoxical phenomenon. People, in watching out for their own personal interests, often feel pressured to bolster their sense of self through the attainment of narcissistic extrinsic aspirations. They comply and conform in striving to achieve those goals.

There is, of course, nothing wrong or weak about wishing—choosing in a free and autonomous fashion—to be part of a group or to be like the other members of a group. It is part of human nature. When well integrated as individuals, people will be solid enough to persist as themselves in a society that is always shifting underfoot, and at the same time, because they draw strength from each other, to cherish their dependence on those others.

PART THREE

How It
All Works

TEN

How to Promote Autonomy

My cousin and her husband are avid gardeners. For six months of each year, their ample yard is in glorious bloom, with more than enough flowers, fruits, and vegetables for them, their neighbors, and the wildlife that is drawn to their property. Gardening is a kind of family affair for them, and from the time their son was two years old he was right beside his parents with his hands in the dirt.

One day when he was in kindergarten, his teacher handed out colored construction paper for the children to make flowers. From the red paper, the children cut circles with rippled edges to represent the blossoms. From the green, they cut stems and leaves. All the children, that is, except my young cousin. He had seen many flowers and knew them well, and he started to make one that looked like what he had seen. He took the red paper and crumpled it up as he began to make the blossom of a red tulip. After all, the flowers he'd seen had all been three-dimensional. His teacher, however, had apparently wanted a two-dimensional flower, pasted to a background. She didn't understand what my young cousin was doing, and she scolded him. He was crestfallen and confused.

That night, at home, when he told his mother what happened, the tears he had successfully choked back in school began to flow. She listened and comforted him, of course, but she faced a dilemma. Obviously, the teacher had been unreasonable. She had been both controlling and evaluative, and she had criticized him for doing something that was as right as what she had expected him to do. Telling her son that his teacher was wrong—a bad teacher, so to speak—would not, however, have been a useful thing for my cousin to do. So, the challenge she faced was to explain to her five-year-old that his idea of how to make a flower was indeed a good one, that there are many ways to make a paper flower, and that sometimes you need to do it the way the teacher wants. The teacher's way was not better, but it was the way she had wanted the flowers this time. My cousin did manage to say all that, and then she got out some paper and they made some three-dimensional flowers together.

R ichard Ryan and I frequently talk to teachers and parents about motivation. Teachers tell us about parents who haven't done a good job of parenting, and parents complain about teachers. There are surely countless incidents like the one with my cousin, where teachers and parents have a different view of things, and the questions we get from teachers or parents often focus on the behavior of the other. Still, we always key our answers to the behavior of the person asking the question. And the answers all boil down to one crucial point: Regardless of how others treat the child, the best thing for you to do is be autonomy supportive. That's also our bottom line when managers and health-care providers ask us about motivation.

Autonomy support is a personal orientation you can take toward other people—particularly other people in a one-down position. This orientation flavors every aspect of your interactions with them. It requires being able to take their perspective—being able to see the world as they see it. It thus allows you to understand why they want what they want and why they do what they do. Simply stated, to be autonomy supportive as, say, a manager means being able to grasp what it is like to be an employee of yours, in your company, community, and industry.

As an autonomy-supportive teacher, parent, or manager, you would be building an alliance with your students, children, or employees, and you would engage new situations from that perspective. This orientation, therefore, pervades all aspects of your teaching, parenting, and managing. Whether the agenda is deciding what to do or evaluating what has been done, carrying out the agenda in an autonomy-supportive way is dramatically different from carrying it out in a more traditional, controlling, or hierarchical way. And the way you carry it out will have an enormous impact on performance, adjustment, and morale.

In the late 1970s, I spent some time observing in public school classrooms. I would sit in the back of the room, watching and listening. The thing that struck me most was how I felt when I left different classrooms. Sometimes I would leave feeling open and light—happy, really. Other times, I would feel closed and heavy, somehow burdened.

I paid careful attention to what the teachers were doing—or more to the point *how* they were doing it—when I felt good, and when I felt not so good. And it seemed to me that when the teachers responded to the children by taking their perspective and encouraging their initiative, I felt good, but when the teachers were demanding and critical, I felt bad. These, of course, were just observations, so Richard Ryan, Louise Sheinman (a school-district administrator), and I decided to collect systematic questionnaire and observational data to test this idea. As we expected, teachers who were oriented toward supporting their students' autonomy had a more positive impact on their students than did the control-oriented teachers. The students of autonomy-supportive teachers were more curious and mastery-oriented, and they evidenced higher self-esteem.

A mother who seemed genuinely convinced of the importance of supporting autonomy in the classroom (and I think at home, as well) once asked me how she would know whether her son's teacher was autonomy supportive in the classroom. I asked whether she ever went to parent-teacher conferences with his teacher, and she said she did. I suggested that she pay attention to how the teacher speaks about her son. Does the teacher take the son's perspective in talking about how he is doing in school? And does it all ring true in terms of what you know about your son? If so, the teacher is probably quite autonomy supportive. If the teacher is able to take the boy's perspective when talking with his mother, it is probable that the teacher would take the boy's perspective when dealing with him.

The idea of autonomy support, of course, seemed fully as relevant to the workplace as to the classroom, so with colleagues Ryan and Connell, I began doing some work in the Xerox Corporation. I traveled to many company offices around the country talking with employees and observing the operations, and we collected questionnaire data from over one thousand people who were involved in the servicing of equipment. In line with our expectations, the data revealed that dynamics very similar to those we had isolated in the classroom were also operative among working adults. Autonomy-supportive managers had workers who were more trusting of the corporation, had less concern about pay and benefits, and displayed a higher level of satisfaction and morale. Furthermore, we confirmed that it was possible to train managers to be more autonomy supportive and, in turn, to elicit more positive work outcomes from the people they supervise.

From all the observations in schools and work organizations, I have concluded that teachers and managers who are autonomy supportive approach many of their functions differently from the way controlling teachers and managers approach them. Here are a few examples.

Deciding What to Do and How to Do It

One of the central features of being autonomy supportive is providing choice, which entails sharing the authority or power of your one-up position. Providing choice can be done at both the individual level and the group level. In other words, part of being autonomy supportive means allowing individuals within your class or work group to participate in making decisions about issues that concern only them, and part is sharing decision making with the group as a whole. The most effective, autonomy-supportive managers and teachers allow their workers or students (whether individually or as a group) to play a role in decision making.

Think about the woman who supervises the design staff for a major department store. Her work group creates the window displays, the decorations throughout the store, the mannequin arrangements within the clothing departments, and so on. The displays are changed at certain times and they follow seasonal themes. As the manager, she could make all the decisions herself, or she could involve her staff in the decision making, both as a group and as individuals. When it is summer, the designs would naturally reflect that season, but there are many summer themes—the beach, hiking, sailing, lawn parties, and so on. The group could decide on the general theme, for example, and individuals could be left to create specific displays—with discussion and coordination among people to ensure a high-quality outcome.

In schools, as well as in the workplace, choice is important. Naturally, students must learn to read, but why not let the group decide what to read? And why not let them talk about how to make the decision—by majority, by consensus, or by committee? The process of decision making is itself an important matter to learn about. Periods could also be built into the class schedule for students to decide individually what to work on—finishing their math assignment, reading another book by an author they like, or whatever.

Although providing choice and encouraging participation in decision making is relevant to decisions about what activities people engage in, there are limits to this. Many managers have told us that there is really no room for their subordinates to choose what gets done—there are things that we just have to do. Many teachers have said much the same thing: The district or the state determines what has to be taught.

Certainly there is some truth to what they say: There are things that must be done. There are tasks that have to be accomplished on the job, and there are subjects that have to be covered in the classroom. But there is almost always some room for deciding what to do, and the point is that truly autonomy-supportive managers or teachers will accept the "givens" and work with them.

Providing choice about how to do a task is even easier than providing choice about what task to do. When a manager's superior dictates what has to be done, the manager still has the possibility of letting the group decide how. With a task that has several aspects, for example, the group could decide how to parcel them out. Suppose a work group has the responsibility of servicing all the copy machines on the north side of the city. Why not let the team members decide how to carve up the region and whether to cover territories as individuals or small groups? Suppose a class of elementary-school students has the task of learning about seeds and plants. Why not let the students decide whether to germinate seeds and grow plants in the classroom, have lectures by the teacher, or have individuals read assignments and then teach each other about what they read? People who are managers or teachers are in the best position to figure out how to provide choice about what to do and how to do it within their own milieu because they are the ones with experience. Examples of how to provide choice are as varied as their imaginations.

Allowing choice about what to do has several possible advantages. For one thing, in the workplace, when the people who will be carrying out a decision participate in making that decision, it is possible that the decisions will be of higher quality than when the manager decides alone. Furthermore, research has confirmed that choice enhances people's intrinsic motivation, so when people participate in decisions about what to do, they will be more motivated and committed to the task—to being sure that the task gets done well. The more seriously people take the challenge of figuring out how to offer choice, the more satisfying they will likely find their jobs, and the more positive will be the responses from their students or employees.

Even people who believe in the power of personal choice may still wonder whether offering choice is always best. The answer is undoubtedly no, and there are a few considerations that have been found to be useful in determining when it is most appropriate to include people in making decisions. One is whether the decision would be too stressful and conflict-promoting if others participated. Suppose there is a team of twelve individuals and the supervisor has been told to downsize by one. It would probably be best for the manager to make that difficult call. The decision is so fraught with potential conflict that asking the group to make the decision could cause hard feelings that would have unpleasant consequences for a long time to come.

Another consideration is whether the particular decision is an appropriate one for people to decide, given their level of maturation. There are some choices, for example, that teenagers would be ready to make, but that are not meaningful or appropriate for young children. It is important for all youngsters to be given choices, but there are some issues that they are not ready to grapple with. A six-year-old who says she wants to baby-sit with her little sister ought not be allowed to (except in a pretend sense), but a twelve-year-old who says she wants to is probably ready.

There may be cases where secrecy is so paramount that subordinates ought not be offered choices. Leaks of critical government information might be the result of including too many people in a decision-making process. Furthermore, there may be cases where the decision to be made has no real impact or relevance to a person, and including him or her may be a waste of resources. There may be cases where a decision needs to be made so quickly that it is not practical to include others. Simply stated, even though offering choices and allowing students, children, and employees to participate in decision making is motivationally (perhaps even morally) desirable, there are various circumstances where it may be impractical or disadvantageous.

Often when Ryan or I give talks or consultations about autonomy support, people tell us that their children, their students, or their employees don't want to have choice—that they want to be told what to do. When we hear such comments, they do ring true, at least to some extent, but we realize that if they are true it is because people have been pushed to that point by being overly controlled in the past.

Remember that if you control people enough, they may begin to act as if they want to be controlled. As a self-protective strategy, they become focused outward—looking for clues about what the people in one-up positions expect of them, looking for what will keep them out of trouble. I have seen this, for example, in countless students who have come to ask what topic to use for their term papers. I typically respond with something like, "What interests you?" only to get the reply, "I don't know; what do you think I should write about?"

A former graduate student in our program, Yasmin Haddad (now a professor at the University of Jordan in Amman), once did a study to help clarify why people might not want to make their own choices. She had elementary-school students work on anagrams. Toward half the students she was very authoritarian, giving them controlling, evaluative feedback about their performance on the anagram task, and toward the other half she was quite supportive, giving them non-evaluative information about their performance. Subsequently, she told all the students that they would be working on four more anagrams, and she asked how many they would like to choose for themselves and how many they would like the experimenter to choose for them. It is interesting that the students with whom she had been controlling, subsequently said they wanted less choice than the students with whom she had been autonomy supportive. It seems that, to some degree at least, people adapt to being controlled and act as if they don't want the very thing that is integral to their nature—namely, the opportunity to be autonomous. They probably fear that they will be evaluated— perhaps even punished—if they make the wrong choice. And they may well be.

Of course, sometimes when teachers and managers tell us that people don't want choice, they are just saying that to justify their own controlling behavior, but sometimes they know what they're talking about. If they are right, however, it is probably because they themselves—or the parents, teachers, or managers the people were previously exposed to—had been controlling and not granted them choice. When people in positions of authority are controlling it is almost as if they were wringing the spirit out of the people they are supposed to be helping.

What all this means is that being autonomy supportive can be very difficult, especially with people who are accustomed to being controlled. Thus, we have to be patient; we have to work with our students or employees to reawaken what is basic to their nature and what will almost surely lead to more positive results. We need to help them get back to the place where they are vital, interested, and eager to take on challenges and responsibilities. We need to promote their autonomy, in part by providing them with choice.

Setting Autonomy-Supportive Limits

I have emphasized repeatedly that supporting autonomy does not mean condoning irresponsibility, nor does it mean allowing people to engage in dangerous or harmful acts. Central to promoting autonomy is encouraging people to understand where their rights end and others' rights begin. Setting limits is a way of communicating that about people's rights and about constraints that exist in the social world. As such, it helps people learn to be responsible in making their choices.

When limits are necessary, there are several important considerations that will help ensure that the limit setting does not undermine autonomy. First, it is possible to have people set their own limits. If an individual's choices might infringe on the rights of others in the group, the group as a whole—rather than its manager or teacher—could discuss the issue and arrive at a set of limits. A. S. Neill, founder of the Summerhill School in England and one of the century's most progressive educators, used this approach very effectively. Students were encouraged to have group discussions aimed at setting their own rules. As long as everyone agreed to it, the decision was considered acceptable.

In many cases, of course, the teachers, managers, or parents need to set the limits. And as the research has shown, the style they use in presenting the limits is important. For example, avoiding controlling language and acknowledging the resistance people may feel facilitate their willingness to accept the limits. Take a routine experience at home in which a mother tells her son, "Have fun playing in the sandbox, but don't throw the sand out into the lawn." The fact of setting such a limit might ruin the son's day, but it needn't. The mother can help her own cause (and the son's) if she leaves out pressuring words and phrases like "do as you should" or "be a good boy." Furthermore, the son will be more likely to play happily without throwing the sand, if his mother acknowledges that she knows he might want to throw the sand all over the place. All of this conveys that she understands his perspective and is not simply trying to push him around.

When people who are being limited understand the reason for limits, they are also more likely to accept them without feeling undermined. If the mother explains to her son why it is important not to throw the sand—for example, it will kill the grass and there will be no sand left in the box for next time—he may be learning something important at the same time that he is being given a meaningful reason to stay within the limit.

The issue of providing useful information, of course, goes far beyond just making limit setting more effective. Understanding the usefulness or importance of the tasks people are doing and of the organization's policies allows people to feel more a part of the organization, less alienated from it. In some cases, particularly in education, it may be useful to go beyond just providing a rationale to encourage people to think for themselves about why a task might be useful for them. Even when students or employees are told what they must do and how they must do it, encouraging them to think through why they are being asked to do it in a particular way can be a valuable problem-solving task. When they fully understand why something is important they will be more willing to do it autonomously.

There are a couple of other important considerations when it comes to setting limits. Making the limits as wide as possible and allowing choice within them will help keep people from feeling so restricted. Setting consequences that are commensurate with the transgression is also an essential element for effective limit setting. Cutting off the hand that goes into the forbidden cookie jar is a bit extreme. When setting limits, people are creating "givens," so it is important to be clear about the consequences of living with the "givens" and the consequences of transgressing them. This issue calls for some thought because once the limits are set and the consequences communicated, it is important to follow through; otherwise, one is undermining one's own credibility.

Consequences of transgressing are not the same thing as punishments. Punishments are a means of controlling people, but limit setting is not about control. It is about encouraging responsibility. If people set appropriate limits and communicate fair consequences, then they can leave it to the student or employee to decide whether to stay within the limits, or to transgress them. It is the person's choice, and if the limit setters are not willing to let him or her make the choice, they are not being truly autonomy supportive. If they get caught in a power struggle, they have moved beyond limit setting in the wrong direction. Setting limits is a matter of being clear and following through; it is not a matter of fighting, pressuring, or struggling.

One of the main purposes of setting limits with children and students is to communicate that life is full of choices and every choice has its consequences. They can choose what they want, but they need to be ready for the consequences. Those are simply the facts of life. Limit setters are working against themselves if they try to force others to comply. Only when the others have *chosen* to stay within the limits will the process be successful, and the process is most likely to succeed when the limit setters can take the others' perspective, minimizing the pressure and keeping the lines of communication open.

Setting Goals and Evaluating Performance

At the beginning of each quarter, many work groups commit to a set of goals that they will attempt to reach in the succeeding months and that will serve as standards against which their performance will later be evaluated. The goals are important for purposes of planning—knowing what are the likely revenues from sales, knowing how many Model C3200's are likely to be produced, and so on—but they are equally important for helping people maintain their motivation.

According to Edward Tolman and Kurt Lewin, two highly influential German émigré psychologists, human behavior is purposive, by which they meant that motivated behavior is directed toward outcomes. People behave when they expect they can attain goals. By aiming for goals, people will remain on track and be able to assess ongoingly whether they are making progress.

To be most effective, goals need to be individualized—they need to be suited specifically to the person who will work toward them—and they need to be set so as to represent an optimal challenge. When they are too easy, the person is likely to be bored and unmotivated; when too difficult, anxious and inefficient.

In setting individual limits, it is important to approach the task from the other person's perspective. I have known many managers who routinely work sixty-hour weeks. They work evening and weekend hours, and they keep very task-focused throughout. For such people, who often have substantial salaries and various perks, their job is challenging, exciting, and rewarding. It is a source of personal fulfillment. But a problem that I have sometimes seen arise is that they expect other employees, such as a secretary or assistant, to be there whenever they need him or her, not grasping that that expectation may be very inappropriate. The other person's life may not allow it, and even if it does, the expectations may still be inappropriate given the circumstances.

The secretary or assistant in all likelihood has a salary far below that of the manager, and the secretary or assistant may have personal commitments during non-eight-to-five hours. In addition, whereas the managers may find the work a source of substantial personal fulfillment, that may not be so for the secretary or assistant. The managers, by failing to take the other's perspective, make unreasonable demands and create inappropriate stresses. Goals and standards must be reasonable, all things considered, for the person to whom they are applied.

The best way to set goals that are optimal for a work group and its members—or for a class and its students—is to involve the people in the process. Being autonomy supportive results in optimal goals that people will commit to because they themselves play an active role in formulating those goals. Through group or individual discussions, the people one supervises or teaches can be encouraged to think about what they are doing, what they ought to be able to accomplish in the weeks or months ahead, what potential obstacles might pop up, and so on. This process is useful in many ways: it leads to optimal goals; it helps people reflect on the way they are doing their jobs; it encourages them to take on new challenges; and it enhances their motivation to attain the goals. And, it provides a standard against which performance can later be appraised.

Evaluating a person's performance is always done against some explicit or implicit standard. People are doing well or poorly only with respect to some set of expectations about how they might be able to do at that time and place. If goals have been properly set, they can represent the standard against which performance is evaluated. The great thing is that if people have participated in setting their goals they can also participate in evaluating their own performance. And who knows better than they how well they have done?

At the end of each school year, I have a meeting with each of my graduate students to talk about the year. I go in with my own opinions about the progress the student has made, and I often have inputs from other faculty members. The meetings usually cover a lot of ground, and at some point during them we get around to what could be considered a performance appraisal. I begin by having the student give me his or her own assessment, and it has amazed me time and time again that the students generally say all the things I have on my mind, and then some. I seldom have much to add. Optimal evaluations are ones where people evaluate their own performance, against standards they set themselves and committed to.

It is important, in any evaluative process, when performance falls short of the standard, to view the situation not as a basis for criticism but as a problem to be solved. In other words, don't jump to immediate conclusions that the cause is in the person's behavior. Perhaps the standards were inappropriate; perhaps unanticipated obstacles came up. And even if the difficulty was caused largely by the person's behavior, viewing it as a problem to be solved—thinking about how this can be improved next time—rather than being critically evaluative will generally produce more positive results.

In a workshop that Ryan once ran in a school district, a fifth-grade teacher was complaining about how she had just been treated by the principal. It seems she had not turned in a report on the previous Friday afternoon—a report that she did not know the purpose of—and on Monday morning the principal really dressed her down, pointing out that her behavior was simply unacceptable.

Ryan presented the problem to the group, inquiring about how they thought the problem should be handled. They had all the right answers. First, they all agreed that in such a situation the principal should step up to the problem. Missing a deadline like that should not go unnoticed, they said. But they added that it would have been very helpful if the principal had let the teacher know ahead of time why the report was so important. The teacher may have been willing to stay longer on Friday, or do it at home Thursday night, if she had understood how important it was.

The group further agreed that it would have been useful not to assume the problem was in her behavior—which it may or may not have been—but instead to be open to understanding what had happened. Maybe an emergency came up on Friday afternoon that took up the time she had set aside to write the report. Even if the problem had been that the teacher simply did not put in the needed effort, a discussion about it rather than a dressing-down would probably have been more productive. Maybe she was feeling overburdened or a bit estranged. Working with her to bring her more on board would likely have had a more positive yield.

It is possible, of course, that the real problem was that there is not adequate communication among the staff in that school. The fact that the teacher did not know the purpose of the report hints at that being true. And if it were true, the principal should be dealing with that issue rather than reproaching the teacher.

Administering Rewards and Recognition

At one point, when I was consultant to a major corporation, I attended a year-end recognition ceremony at a regional office in Texas. There were numerous, substantial awards—large-screen televisions, microwaves, blocks of tickets to professional football games, and so on—and each was given either to an individual or a team that did best on some criterion. It was rather programmed and predictable, but it did seem festive.

Still, I couldn't help thinking that this was not the best way to deal with recognition. Each award was given to the person or team who won some competition, which means that the process turned people against each other when it would have been better to encourage them to work together. Furthermore, with a competition, the second-place person—who may have missed out only by a hair—is a loser. Competitions are typically all or none, which means that many superb performers become losers. A team that is second or third (out of, say, eight) on every single criterion wins nothing, even though in a sense they may be the best overall performers of the year.

"Why not give each team an award for *its* most important accomplishment, or for *its* biggest improvement?" I ask the branch manager afterward. That way, teams compete against themselves, rather than each other, and each team can be a winner. Of course, this strategy is not intended as a means of motivating employees, but rather is a means of expressing appreciation to each team for its year of work. If some team has not been having a good year, that is something to be addressed ongoingly. But making them a loser at the recognition meeting, when the purpose is to promote good feelings for the group as a whole, is not likely to help.

Rewards and recognition are important, but as the research has so clearly shown and I have reiterated many times, when rewards or awards are used as a means of motivating people, they are likely to backfire. Watches to employees and gold stars to students can enhance their sense of competence and leave them feeling acknowledged and appreciated. But the use of rewards is a treacherous road to travel, and one has to be very careful—and truthful—about why and how they are being used.

Recognizing the Obstacles

The fact that most teachers, managers, and parents do less supporting autonomy and offering choice than would be optimal, leads to the question of why this is so. No doubt some people in one-up positions have personalities that are oriented toward controlling others rather than being supportive—the authoritarian personality, for example—and that represents one difficult problem. But there are other obstacles to autonomy support that are both bigger and easier to change. One obstacle is that some people do not have the skills necessary for practicing autonomy support. They need training.

In our research at Xerox, we did a training intervention to teach one group of managers how to be more sensitive and responsive to their subordinates, how to promote initiative and responsibility, and how to provide choice and support. The intervention began with a two-day off-site workshop and continued with occasional meetings, discussions, and feedback sessions over the succeeding three months.

Prior to the intervention, and then again after, we assessed their managerial approach on a scale that ranged from highly controlling to highly autonomy supportive, and we found that the managers had indeed become more autonomy supportive during the period of training. More important, perhaps, we found that during the same period the employees of these managers became more positive in their perceptions and attitudes about the workplace. The training had an impact on both the managers who had been trained and the employees they supervised.

Controlling personalities and lack of skills in teachers and managers are not the only obstacles to facilitating autonomy-supportive behavior, however. The situation can also make it very difficult to be autonomy supportive. Over and over, teachers have told us that they began their careers with excitement and enthusiasm, eager to work with the students to facilitate their intellectual and personal development. But as the years passed and the pressures and demands intensified, the teachers have said, they lost much of their enthusiasm. They point to standardized curricula, where they have to teach specified material rather than what seemed right to them, and to the pressures on them to be sure their students get high standardized achievement scores.

It occurred to us that these kinds of pressures may actually make the teachers more controlling—they feel pressured, so in turn they pressure the students. We did an experiment to test this hypothesis. We had subjects come into the lab to teach students how to solve problems. We gave the teachers plenty of time to practice with the problems, and we gave them both a list of useful hints and the actual solutions to all the problems. The teachers had been randomly assigned to one of two groups, and everything was the same for the two groups except for the fact that we made one additional statement to the teachers in one group. We said, "Remember, it is your responsibility as a teacher to make sure your students perform up to high standards."

We tape-recorded the teaching session that followed, and later we analyzed the teaching styles. The results were astonishing. Teachers to whom we had mentioned "performing up to high standards" spent twice as much time talking during the teaching session as the other teachers. They also made three times as many directives and three times as many controlling statements (e.g., using words like "should" and "must").

In a way, it is all quite ironic. Parents, politicians, and school administrators all want students to be creative problem-solvers and to learn material at a deep, conceptual level. But in their eagerness to achieve these ends, they pressure teachers to produce. The paradox is that the more they do that, the more controlling the teachers become, which, as we have seen so many times, undermines intrinsic motivation, creativity, and conceptual understanding in the students. The harder the teachers are pushed to get results, the less likely it is that the important results will be forthcoming. The same is true for managers and others in one-up positions. The more they feel pressured to get results from their employees (or children, or athletes, or students) the harder they push. Unfortunately, in the process, they typically sabotage their own efforts.

Although the experiment was done with teachers, it really has relevance to anyone in a one-up position. When parents or managers feel more pressured, it is also more difficult for them to be autonomy supportive. Controlling others seems to be the sort of "knee-jerk" reaction to feeling stress in any one-up position, and it is likely to have negative ramifications. One of the most important implications of this is that people in such positions—teachers, parents, and managers, for example—will not be very effective in supporting the autonomy of their students and employees if they do not have their own support. Finding that support—finding a network of people who will help you satisfy your own needs for autonomy, competence, and relatedness—is one of the most important aspects of promoting autonomy in the people you teach, care for, or supervise. We return to this point in Chapter Twelve.

ELEVEN

Promoting Healthy Behavior

C aroline was severely obese when she went to her intake interview for a physician-supervised diet program. A thirty-nine-year-old mother of two, Caroline seemed very agitated. She said she really had to lose weight—that it was very important to her—and when the interviewer asked her why, she burst into tears. Several minutes passed with no words, and then she opened her purse and took out a photo of a stunning woman who appeared to be in her mid-twenties. "That's what I looked like sixteen years ago when I got married," she said. "Now my husband says that if I don't lose at least one hundred pounds he's going to leave me."

Victoria, who was about the same age and size as Caroline, also interviewed for the program. She was more relaxed and her story was quite different. She said she had been gaining weight fairly steadily for six or eight years. During stressful periods at work and in her extended family, she said, she ate continually. She had been thinking about this a lot over the preceding six months, and she had made a clear decision that she was ready to take charge of her health. She had made up her mind to eat less and avoid unhealthy foods, and she was ready to begin exercising regularly. She wanted to start with a low-calorie diet and to consult with an exercise physiologist.

The contrast between these two women is startling. Caroline was there because of external pressures, while Victoria was there because she had made a personal commitment to change. It is thus highly probable that the two would be differentially successful in the program, that Victoria's efforts would be more likely to result in maintained weight loss. In fact, my colleagues and I have recently been exploring the very issue contained within this story in a program of research on how to promote healthy behavior change. We have investigated, for example, whether people's reasons for entering a weight-loss program, an alcohol treatment program, or a smoking-cessation program will predict how successful they will be in the program.

There is no longer any question that there are serious health risks associated with severe obesity, yet millions of Americans have failed to regulate their eating and exercise. There is likewise no question that there are serious health risks associated with tobacco use, yet millions of Americans continue to smoke. Indeed, many Americans regularly engage in a variety of unhealthy behaviors, or fail to engage in healthy ones.

If obituaries told the full story of people's deaths, more than half of them would point out that the person ". . . ended his (or her) life prematurely." The phrase would not be intended to imply suicide, in the conventional sense, but rather to highlight the fact that behavior, and the psychosocial factors that influence it, are important contributors to death. A recent study by physician-researchers J. Michael McGinnis and William Foege, for example, indicates that tobacco and alcohol use, and exercise and diet patterns, account for more than one-third of all American deaths, typically by triggering the onset of terminal illnesses such as cancer and cardiovascular disease. People are "behaving themselves to death," so to speak, and yet the obituaries report only the illnesses—the cancers or heart attacks—as the causes of their deaths.

In part because of the known seriousness of the health risks from tobacco use and obesity, smoking cessation and dieting have become big business. *The New York Times* best-seller list frequently includes a diet book; smoking-cessation programs have proliferated, with some people having participated in several; and belonging to a health club is de rigueur in some circles. All this suggests that people have

some understanding of the risks and benefits of various health-re-
lated activities, so they make efforts to change. But the results are
generally dismal. A smoking-cessation program is considered successful, if something like ten percent of the participants are able to
maintain long-term abstinence. And maintenance of weight loss over
a period of three to four years following a diet program is a rarity.

After years of studying motivation in the laboratory, as well as in
homes, schools, and businesses, Richard Ryan and I were ready to
begin exploring the motivational issues involved in promoting
healthy behavior. At that time, Geoffrey Williams was a young internist and faculty member at the University of Rochester Medical
School. He had become interested in the psychological meaning of
interactions between doctors and their patients because he was dis-
satisfied about the way many of his patients expected him to solve
their medical problems but then failed to carry through on what he
prescribed. He joined forces with us, and we began to explore why so
many people do not adhere to medical regimens and are unsuccessful
in their attempts to lose weight, stop smoking, limit their alcohol
consumption, and so on.

The Reasons for Change

When we began, we decided to focus on the reasons why people
enter programs designed to change self-destructive behaviors. Ryan
and colleagues did the first of these studies in an alcohol treatment
program, while Williams and colleagues did the next in a clinic-
based weight-loss program. We had developed a survey instrument
called the Treatment Self-Regulation Questionnaire, which asks participants a series of questions about why they are entering the program.

Our interest was in how autonomous or self-determined each
patient was in entering the program, so the questions all had that
focus. Some were concerned with external factors that might pres-

sure people into participation—factors such as their friends' or spouses' insisting they go. Those are the most controlling, least autonomous types of reasons. Some questions focused on introjected reasons for attending—things like being ashamed of their obesity, feeling like a bad person for being an alcoholic, or thinking they *should* change. These reasons were still quite controlling, for in these cases the people were being pressured and coerced by their own inner thoughts. It is no doubt better for them to be pressuring themselves than to be pressured by others, but our past research in other domains had indicated that it is only when people fully endorse a change—only when they have a kind of relaxed commitment, reflecting a deep personal choice to change—that they will behave autonomously and will have a higher probability of being successful in their attempts to change. People with autonomous reasons for entering the programs were ones who were ready to take charge of their own drinking or eating behaviors because they were tired of having dulled senses, hangovers, and stressful relationships caused by alcohol abuse, or of feeling sluggish and having trouble moving around caused by severe obesity. They were simply ready to improve the quality of their own lives.

It seems so logical, so natural—indeed, so survival-oriented—for people to limit their alcohol intake, to diet and exercise, to give up smoking. And yet many people continue their unhealthy behavior. One might wonder, therefore, why all participants in treatment programs aren't ready to take charge of their drinking and eating behaviors, and more generally why people are not fully willing to be autonomously self-regulating of behaviors that will make them healthier.

The reason, quite simply, is that abusing alcohol, as well as smoking and overeating, all serve a purpose. They bind anxiety, provide an escape from pressures, or provide some other, similar type of comfort. Drinking may dampen people's feelings of loneliness, for example; eating may allow people to avoid their fears of rejection; and smoking may help people tolerate the nervousness they feel when they encounter a group of people in a social setting. Each of these behaviors can serve many different purposes which make them resistant to change.

Consider, for example, the man—an advertising executive in his early thirties—who uses alcohol to get a boost on those infrequent occasions when he feels depressed, but who also uses it to calm down when he has gotten overstimulated by a stressful day at work. In fact, for him, alcohol is a seductive and multipurpose palliative for any mood swing. When he walks into a party and feels too self-conscious to speak, he has a drink or two and becomes voluble, even funny. When he is waiting to hear about some project he has turned in to his boss, he finds that a drink helps him tolerate the uncertainty. When he has a date or a meeting but doesn't feel quite up to it, he also finds that a drink helps.

Sometimes when he is alone, especially on those difficult mornings when his hangover is intense, he has the uneasy feeling that he is overusing alcohol and that it may have some long-term costs. Indeed, on many such mornings he has resolved to quit. But the resolve is fragile and lasts only until he feels those uncomfortable feelings—the depression, overstimulation, self-consciousness, or dread—making their reappearance.

To be ready to change self-destructive behaviors, people have to reach the point where they are willing to allow the feelings that the behaviors are blocking. People must be ready to feel the frightening sense of inadequacy, the painful fear of abandonment, the terror of their mortality, or whatever it is that continues to power the unhealthy behaviors. They also have to be willing to "feel different" from others when they drink seltzer at a party where everyone else is drinking liquor; they have to be ready to resist the rich desserts that are put on the table in front of them; and they have to be willing to get up and go jogging when they would rather sit and watch television.

When people are ready to accept responsibility—responsibility of the deepest and most profound type—for the behaviors that are so directly related to their well-being, the returns are likely to be great. In the study of alcohol treatment done by Ryan and colleagues, par-

ticipants who were truly doing it for themselves—who endorsed autonomous reasons rather than controlling ones—attended the program more regularly. They stuck with it rather than dropping out.
Similarly, in the weight-loss study by Williams and colleagues, patients whose reasons for attending were more autonomous not only
attended more of the weekly meetings during the six-month, very-
low-calorie-diet program, but they lost more weight during that period and had maintained more of their losses at a two-year
follow-up. These people had really decided to make a change; they
were integrated and autonomous in the way they engaged the process of making a change that was important for their own health.
And they achieved concrete results that will prevent illness and promote well-being.

Of course, there are also *physiological* processes involved in
some of the counterproductive behaviors. People become physiologi-
cally addicted to alcohol and nicotine, for example, and recent evidence suggests that there may be a genetic predisposition to obesity.
But these physiological processes do *not* cause the behaviors in a
direct sense, because the relevant behaviors are also influenced by
psychological processes. People with addictions or with genetic
predispositions may find it harder to change than will those who
don't have to counteract such forces, but people *can* break addictions and they *can* overcome genetic predispositions when they are
really ready to do so. When people are ready to accept responsibility
for their behavior and health—when they are ready to make a deep
personal commitment and to accept the uncomfortable feelings that
may accompany change—their efforts to change are likely to be successful.

People's success at changing behavior begins with their taking
genuine interest in their own motivations. This means asking themselves why they are trying to change, and thinking honestly about
their answers. If the reasons they come up with are that other people
are pressuring them, or that they think they should change in order
to live longer, or that they want to match some image, then they are
off to a bad start. These reasons are not very convincing, and they are

not likely to motivate meaningful change because they lack a personal endorsement.

Recall the advertising executive who resolved to change only when the hangovers got too bad. His reasons were superficial and reflected no personal commitment, so his resolve to change amounted to naught. Indeed, if I had heard him give such a reason, I would have thought, "No sense bothering to try."

In contrast, think of the woman who began smoking in her early teens because all of her friends were doing it and she thought it helped her look grown-up and sexy. She became quite dependent on her cigarettes, and by the time she was twenty-one, she smoked three packs a day. She had tried to stop a couple of times, with no more success at quitting tobacco than the advertising executive who occasionally "gave up" drinking. But then something happened for this young woman that changed all that. She fell in love with an attractive, outgoing man with plans and dreams. He was a nonsmoker, and although he did not prod her about her own smoking, he represented an example for her. And even more, as she began thinking about their life together, with babies growing into adults, she began to think of how her smoking could hurt them as well as herself. She, in fact, stopped smoking, and although it was not easy, it did last. Why? Because she had found a truly meaningful personal reason, and when she did, she had a deep determination to carry through.

The decision to change is one that individuals must make for themselves. That means exploring why they want to change and also paying attention to the benefits they are getting from the behavior. By exploring their motivations, people will be in a position to make a true choice. The choice might be to change, but it might also be to continue the behavior. It is up to them. But until they take interest in their underlying motivations and make a real choice, the self-destructive behaviors will continue to "control them."

Explorations of one's motivation can be a difficult process, and carrying out a true choice can also be difficult. But these are the starting points for successful change.

Noncompliance with Medical Regimens

One of many significant problems facing the medical establishment today is what typically goes under the rubric of noncompliance. An extraordinarily large percentage of people fail to take their medications as prescribed. They take too much, or too little. They forget it for a day or two; they remember sometimes but not others; or they just don't bother. Such noncompliance has a whole range of consequences. It allows the illness to progress, causing greater health-care costs; it leads to stronger (often more toxic) medical prescriptions; and it can be confusing to physicians who believe the medication should be having positive effects.

Noncompliance is also a problem in medical research. If someone is prescribed a medication as part of an important clinical study but then fails to take the medicine as prescribed, it could invalidate the test. And if these people lie and say they followed the prescription, it can lead to the accumulation of inaccurate medical conclusions and have potentially harmful effects on other patients.

Poor compliance with medical regimens has led many health-care providers to take a heavy-handed approach with their patients—to be highly authoritarian and to use a variety of scare tactics. And still the problem remains.

Our approach to this problem is quite different from the controlling stance adopted by many. Indeed, we do not even formulate this issue as one of *compliance.* Compliance conveys the sense of being a "pawn"; it conveys the sense of doing something because others told you to. Using the term can thus strengthen the view that "encouraging people to behave in health-promoting ways" is a matter of controlling their behavior—of making them comply. Our view, instead, is that people will adhere to a medication prescription if they feel autonomous in doing it, if their reasons for doing it are their own, if they accept responsibility for getting better.

In a recent study, Williams, with psychologist Gail Rodin and others, assessed the reasons why patients take their medication. These were all patients who had been on long-term medication regimens for a variety of illnesses such as angina, postmenopausal symptoms, and hypertension. Some patients endorsed reasons that were very controlling—they take their medicine because their doctor told them they should. Others endorsed reasons that were more autonomous—they take their medicine because it is important to them personally to be healthy. The patients' medication taking was then followed over the next two weeks, and the data indicated that those patients who did it for themselves—who were autonomous in their reasons—were much more reliable in following the prescriptions. Their doctors had made the prescriptions, but they, the patients, had accepted full responsibility for adhering to them. The prescriptions had come from the doctors, but once people had accepted them, adherence was not a problem.

Accepting responsibility, once again, involves people taking interest in their own motivation. Quite simply, it means thinking about whether they believe in the utility of the medication and deciding whether they want to get well badly enough that they are willing to exert the effort or devise supports to help them. Again, it is their choice. If they do believe in the value of the prescription, and if they do decide that being well is worth the effort, then adherence is likely to follow.

Supporting Patients' Autonomy

When I first moved to Rochester, I needed an internist, so I asked around for a referral. Someone gave me a name, and I checked it out with other people who told me they had heard he was good. I made an appointment for a physical exam as a way of getting started. From that initial visit, I was uncomfortable with his interpersonal style. The differential in status was somehow made eminently clear:

He was one-up and I was one-down. At one point, he made a deroga-
tory remark about one of his staff members who had not done something quickly enough, and I winced. His communications were full of
judgments of right or wrong and good or bad, and he was firm in
telling me what I should and should not do. I felt constricted in his
presence, and I didn't ask any questions. I not only withheld the one
or two questions I had, but the other questions that concerned me
didn't even come to mind until after I left his office.

I remember one occasion some while after the initial visit when I
was sick, and I felt reluctant to call my doctor. I went round and
round in my own head about whether I should or should not call. I
never did, and fortunately in a few days I felt fine again. But what if
my problem had been a more serious one? The remarkable thing to
me, as I reflect on it, is that although I was a young adult at the time,
I had gotten caught up in a relationship where I was, in essence,
acting like a child. In response to the doctor's critical, authoritarian
style, I had regressed.

The contrast of my reaction to this physician and my reaction to
the dentist I had when I lived in Palo Alto was startling. On my first
visit to him I was seated in a chair that looked out a large window
into a courtyard that held a century-old oak tree. I felt immediately
comforted. Then the doctor came in wearing a Hawaiian print shirt
rather than a white smock, and he introduced himself using his first
name. His assistants, while clearly respectful, also called him by his
first name. Questions came easily to me, and his answers had all the
information I was seeking. I left the first appointment thinking he
was a great dentist. I did not feel "one-down," even though I had
substantial respect for his expertise and his authority. I started floss-
ing more regularly, and I felt that I could call on him if I needed him.

From my experiences with these two health-care providers, it
seemed clear that the doctors' orientations toward their patients
must have a substantial effect on the patients, and it seemed to me
that the style used by my Palo Alto dentist was the better of the two.
Later, after years of research on motivation, I had the language to use

in describing these two health-care providers. The former was clearly controlling and the latter, autonomy supportive. And all of our past research led to the prediction, which eventually we would test, that the autonomy-supportive style would not only feel better to most patients (as it did to me), but that it would also have positive motivational consequences.

Williams, Ryan, and I have conducted several investigations to explore whether patients' perceptions of practitioners' having an autonomy-supportive (versus a controlling) style actually affects the patients' motivation and health status. For example, in the weight-loss study mentioned earlier, we assessed patients' perceptions of the staff. We found that when the staff was perceived as more autonomy supportive, the patients reported more autonomous reasons for adhering to the program guidelines, which, in turn, predicted maintained weight loss over a two-year period. Patients' being autonomous—being truly self-regulating—which is essential for behaving in healthy ways, actually appears to be influenced by the way health-care providers relate to them.

We found the same results in the medication-adherence study. Patients' perceptions of their doctors' being autonomy supportive were related to the patients' endorsing of more autonomous or integrated reasons for taking their medication, which, in turn, related to greater adherence. These and other studies confirm that when health-care providers recognize the importance of psychosocial factors for patients' health and thus relate to patients in more autonomy-supportive ways, the patients are likely to become more autonomous in their motivation and to behave in healthier ways over the long haul.

People sometimes ask how they can tell if their doctor is autonomy supportive. The answer, really, is quite straightforward. Pay attention to how you feel when you leave the doctor's office. Do you feel constricted, one-down, and passive, as I did when I left that internist's office? Or do you feel comforted and respected, as I did when I left my dentist's?

The Biopsychosocial Approach

Throughout the twentieth century, the American medical profession has increasingly focused on the technical aspects of health care, subscribing to a viewpoint called the biomedical approach. Illness is addressed in biological terms, viewed as being caused by germs or organ malfunctioning, and it is treated by medication and surgical interventions. The narrow specializations that have become so common—orthopedists who work only on wrists, or internists who treat only kidney problems—are a natural outcome of the biomedical approach. Focusing on the technical aspects leads one to specialize in order to be a true expert. With the concern for biological causes and cures, doctors have become oriented toward treating organs rather than people. The patients, in turn, have often felt that they are not being related to by their doctors and that they are not getting the information they need to manage their own health care. The highly technical focus has thus widened the gulf between the expert doctors who are the prescribers and the patients who are expected to comply with the doctors' orders.

Although many doctors feel quite comfortable with the biomedical model and conduct their practices accordingly, a growing number have felt vaguely uneasy with the impersonality of modern medicine. These doctors long for the personal care provided by the general practitioners of, say, the 1950s, coupled, of course, with the medical knowledge of the 1990s.

The Medical Center at the University of Rochester has for a quarter of a century been a leading advocate of an alternative viewpoint referred to as the biopsychosocial approach. Illness is understood as having many facets that involve an interplay of natural systems, including chemical, neurological, psychological, and social. Because changes at any one level lead reciprocally to changes at others, every level is a contributor to human illness and health. Hans Selye's pioneering work showed, for example, that stress can affect all the organs of the body by overactivating the autonomic nervous system. Indeed, various psychological states can lead to physiological changes such as excess glandular secretions, rigidity in the musculature, and suppression of the immune system, all of which have been implicated in the onset of cancer, heart disease, diabetes, and other of the illnesses that are responsible for the majority of American deaths.

It is clear, then, that psychological and interpersonal factors can directly affect people's health by influencing somatic functioning. But equally as important, psychosocial factors can also indirectly affect people's health by affecting their behavior. Both the psychological and interpersonal processes described in this book that are related to human motivation and autonomy influence the behaviors that affect physical as well as mental health.

High-risk behaviors such as overeating, smoking, abusing alcohol, eating unhealthy foods, taking foolish risks behind the wheel, having unprotected casual sex, and playing with firearms, for example, have motivational underpinnings—they are psychologically and socially determined. Friends are doing it, so you cannot refuse. Your vulnerable ego pushes you to do it. Your inner turmoil seems too great to bear, and the behavior distracts you from that turmoil. Authorities have warned against it, so the tendency to defy controls makes you want to do it. Each of these motivational reasons suggests that when people are less autonomous—that is, when they are more controlled—they are more likely to engage in the behaviors that promote ill-being.

Similarly, the factors that lead people to change these unhealthy behaviors are also motivational, as our research has repeatedly indicated. Recall the study by Williams and colleagues, showing that people were more successful in losing weight and maintaining the losses over a two-year period when their motivation was autonomous rather than controlled—when they were doing it for themselves rather than for others. In general, then, when people are more autonomous—when they are more intrinsically motivated and have integrated the regulation of important behaviors—they will not only be less likely to engage in high-risk behaviors in the first place, but they will be more able to change those behaviors if they have gotten hooked by them.

The biopsychosocial approach to treatment emphasizes building a partnership between health-care providers and their patients. It recognizes the importance of providers' treating the whole person, and it recognizes that social and psychological processes are integral to well-being. Thus, for example, the approach emphasizes that the way a provider relates to a patient can influence whether the patient behaves in healthy ways—taking medication, losing weight, stopping smoking, and so on.

Providers encourage patients to be active in managing their health—to ask questions and to participate in arriving at workable solutions to health-care problems. Doctors, of course, provide valuable information and offer suggestions about treatment plans, but patients are encouraged to think about the options and to play a role in deciding on the plan. Behaviors are not prescribed by the provider; instead, the partnership makes a joint decision. That way, patients will not only offer valuable insights—it is the patients, not the providers, who know what the patients will be able to do—but they will be more motivated to carry out the plans. It has long been recognized in all domains of human activity that when people play a role in deciding what to do and how to do it, they will be more committed to carrying through on the decision.

All of the features of being autonomy supportive—taking the other's perspective, offering choice, providing relevant information that the other person may have no access to, giving the rationale for suggestions or requests, acknowledging the other's feelings, and minimizing the use of controlling language and attitudes—describe perfectly what it means to be psychosocial or patient-centered in the practice of medicine. They help to build partnerships, and they are the physician attitudes and behaviors that are espoused by the biopsychosocial approach.

To build partnerships in health care thus involves the providers' being autonomy supportive and taking the patients' perspectives.

Accordingly, our studies on how doctors' orientations toward patients—whether they are autonomy supportive or controlling—affect the patients' motivation and health helped to validate the biopsychosocial approach for promoting healthy behavior change.

Responsibility and Autonomy Support

When providers are autonomy supportive, they are more likely to understand and accept why a patient would be smoking, drinking, or overeating. And with that understanding they will be able to work with the patients to develop treatment plans that are likely to succeed. Treatment plans that are imposed from a doctor's perspective, that don't take account of a patient's unique needs and the obstacles the patient experiences, are likely to fail. Remember the example of the woman who failed to take her hypertension medication when her doctor was controlling but became quite reliable about it after she switched to an autonomy-supportive doctor?

Ultimately, a patient's behavior (and thus the patient's health) is his or her own responsibility. Short of heroic efforts like forcibly hospitalizing and medicating patients, doctors cannot make a patient well if the patient is not willing to cooperate. Patients have the right to smoke, and if they decide to, even though both they and the doctors know it is harmful, doctors need to respect their decision. Doctors cannot stop patients from doing it, and in most cases, when doctors cross the line from adviser to controller they have gone too far. They have usurped a responsibility that belongs to the patient.

Although a patient's health behavior is his or her own responsibility, doctors do have the responsibility of encouraging a patient to behave in healthy ways. It is thus a fine line that physicians must walk, promoting healthy behavior without controlling it. To do that, it is important for doctors to provide information to patients—for example, the information that nicotine exacerbates hypertension and that this patient is particularly susceptible to those effects. It is also important for them to speak about health risks, and encourage change—in an autonomy-supportive way—by conveying the message that they are concerned with the patient's well-being and are there to help. But when they go too far, when they begin to control, it is likely to backfire.

I heard the story of a cantankerous seventy-two-year-old chain-smoker who lived his last years in Florida. For years, doctors had warned him to stop smoking, for if he did not, they said, cigarettes would surely take his life. Well, when the end came, it was a brain tumor that got him, and he said he had shown those doctors after all. But it is not as easy as that. He resisted, he said, because he found the doctors too controlling. But he paid for his defiance. Cigarettes did not end his life, but they did diminish the quality of the last several years. It was the cigarettes that had him coughing up phlegm each morning and panting heavily when he climbed stairs or walked up a small hill.

Of course, I do not place all the blame on the doctors. The man could have decided to stop smoking and improved his own life. And I could have behaved more maturely in response to my first Rochester internist. Doctors' styles surely have an effect on their patients, but the patients can rise above it, as we will see in the next chapter. I could have been more active in asking questions and more assertive in getting what I needed. But I did not accept responsibility for myself and my own health care, and it took me a while before I began to explore my own motivations and to act in a more self-determined way.

People's health-relevant behavior is thus an interaction of their own motivations and of the style of the health-care providers. For more positive outcomes, people could explore their own motivations to find a true desire to behave in healthy ways, and the American medical establishment could become more autonomy supportive.

Training Providers to Be Autonomy Supportive

Because doctors' being autonomy supportive is important for promoting health in their patients, it seemed to Williams and me that exploring how doctors could be trained to be more autonomy supportive and patient-centered would be a worthy endeavor. We gained access to the second-year students in two medical schools who were taking a medical interviewing course. That is the place where aspiring physicians learn how to relate to their patients—how to give and get relevant information. At the beginning of the course, we assessed both the students' reasons for taking the course, to ascertain how autonomous they were in their motivation, and their attitudes about the psychosocial approach. At the end of the five-month course, we assessed the same variables, along with the students' perceptions of the autonomy-supportiveness of their instructors. There were over twenty instructors at the two universities, and they varied greatly in the extent to which they were autonomy supportive versus controlling in their teaching style.

Results showed that the students whose instructors were autonomy supportive in their teaching approach became more autonomous in their reasons for studying interviewing and doctor-patient communications. In turn, as they became more autonomous in their own learning behavior, they also developed more positive attitudes about the biopsychosocial approach. In essence, the instructors who supported their students' autonomy encouraged the internalization and integration of psychosocial values.

A few months later, the students were audiotaped while interviewing a simulated patient, and the results of the tape analysis indicated that the medical students who had become more autonomous in their own motivation, and who had integrated the value of the psychosocial approach, were more "patient-centered" than those who had not. They supported the patient's autonomy.

One of the most interesting things about the medical-student study was the finding that an autonomy-supportive teaching style led the students to adopt a more autonomy-supportive style of interacting with patients. In fact, when one draws together all of the research referred to in this book, one discovers that being a good parent, a good teacher, a good manager, or a good health-care provider all have something in common, namely, an autonomy-supportive interpersonal style. Indeed, being successful in any one-up position, as it relates to the performance, development, and well-being of people in a one-down position, begins with an autonomy-supportive interpersonal style. It begins with listening openly so you can understand the situation from the other's perspective.

TWELVE

Being Autonomous Amidst the Controls

America is replete with its legends—with its Abe Lincolns who, against all odds, rose to greatness. More than legends, actually, these people are models of self-reliance. Lincoln, after all, transcended his impoverished surroundings by educating himself when formal education was not available to him.

Today, as well, one finds countless people who were raised in poverty and neglect in our inner cities or rural countrysides and who go on to distinguished careers—or, remarkable in its own right, to stable, satisfying lives, providing for their children what was not provided for them and contributing to their community with a spirit of gratitude and hope.

Even though people's motivation, behavior, and well-being are powerfully influenced by their social environments, it is fascinating that some people are able to fare quite admirably despite having experienced an upbringing marked by pressures, chaos, abuse, or neglect. How is one to account for this seeming puzzle?

To begin with, one must recognize that people are born with individual differences. On every human characteristic (height, intelligence, aggressiveness, or whatever), people have the predisposition not only to differ from each other, but to do so in accord with what is called a normal distribution—the familiar bell-shaped curve. This means that before the environment has had any effect on them, people have their starting place on each human dimension.

Each of these dimensions has its average—what is technically called the mean. There is a mean height and a mean IQ, for example, and most people are clustered around the mean. As you get further from the mean there are fewer cases. For example, the mean IQ is about 100, and two-thirds of all people have IQs between 90 and 110. In contrast, only about two percent of the population have IQs in the range from 120 to 140, and a comparable two percent fall between 60 and 80.

There is ample evidence that children are born with individual differences on psychological as well as physical variables, and these are the ones that are critical for the question we are addressing. Considerable research has documented, for example, that there are innate differences in temperament. Some infants are personable and happy; others are withdrawn and irritable. Some are vital and active; others are anergic and passive. These qualities of vitality and proactivity are, of course, related to intrinsic motivation.

The more vital and proactive children are, the better start they have in developing an autonomous self-assured presence. But that's just the beginning. Immediately, the environment begins affecting these processes, facilitating healthy development if it allows satisfaction of one's basic needs, and diminishing development if it does not. This, of course, suggests that children who are raised in impoverished environments will fare worse than those raised in nurturing environments. But it still leaves the question of why some are able to do rather well in spite of these environmental influences.

Finding a Special Support

Some children who live in what are generally non-nurturing environments are able to find an adult with whom to have a special relationship. This is no doubt particularly true for children who are engaging and proactive to begin with. Very often, individuals who have risen above difficult backgrounds tell the story of some person who truly believed in them and gave them the support they needed to believe in themselves. Sometimes the person is a relative; sometimes it is a teacher or coach. Whoever it is, if children are able to attract the ongoing support of a special person who really believes in them, they may rise above the influence of their general surroundings. And if they are children with exceptional, innate characteristics to begin with, the likelihood is even greater.

I was told the story of a school superintendent—I'll call him Robert—who grew up in a very poor neighborhood. He had a brother and a sister, but he never saw his father. His mother struggled to keep the family together by cleaning houses, but that meant she was seldom at home. His descriptions of the schools he attended sound like a nightmare.

Robert lives in comfortable suburban surroundings, has two children who seem to enjoy their lives, and belongs to several volunteer organizations. Stories of his boyhood include a couple of noteworthy points about significant people. When he was a boy, his grandmother lived only two blocks away, and they had a very special attachment. She stayed with him when he was very young, and later she helped him with his homework. His stories also make frequent mention of a man who was athletic director at the settlement house in his neighborhood. Robert was particularly good at basketball, and joined in other sporting activities as well. The man was married, with his own family, and Robert spent quite a bit of time with them. I suspect that these two special relationships were powerful influences that allowed Robert to actualize what were obviously special talents.

Individuals and Their Social World

Of course, everyone in impoverished or coercive surroundings does not have the advantage of such special relationships, but people do have the possibility of positively affecting their social world, as well as being affected by it. I have emphasized repeatedly that controlling versus autonomy-supportive contexts have profound effects that can persist throughout people's lives, influencing their motivation, behavior, and development. But to some extent, people influence the social world that influences them, and one very important implication of this is that children who are personable, vital, and proactive, for example, are likely to draw the best out of their caregivers. By being more vital and engaging, children can elicit greater involvement and autonomy support from the same parents and teachers who are colder and more controlling with other children. That little extra autonomy support can give these children an added boost.

Thus, children's innate characteristics not only affect their behavior and development directly, but these characteristics also have an effect on the social environment that in turn affects the children's development. Social environments have their own stable characteristics, but the fact that people can have even a small influence on their social environments helps to explain how some have been able to emerge from those environments with a more positive demeanor.

One often hears teachers say that it is easy to support the autonomy of students who are engaging and proactive, but passive or aggressive children just seem to ask for control. And when children do pull for control, it is easy to fall into the trap of controlling them, which further hinders their development. Take the case of two children—one who was a bit more passive than average and another who was a bit more proactive than average—who entered the same classroom. Both had the same teacher, whose ongoing style was a bit on the controlling side. When it came to these two children, she treated them slightly differently, being a little more controlling with the former and a little more autonomy supportive with the latter. As she saw it, the first child needed more control, whereas the second was more able to take responsibility for himself. Naturally, these differential interpersonal contexts provided for the two children by the same teacher in the same classroom affected the two children differently, so by the end of the school year, the children were more different than they had been at the beginning. The first child was even more passive, and the second, more autonomous. Their relative positions on the bell-shaped curve had changed.

As development proceeds, people build expectations about the social context. For example, if a girl had lived for her first five years in a very controlling home, she would probably enter school expecting it to be very controlling also, and to some extent, she would act as if it were.

Think of a work situation in which two different people work at the same job, with a manager who treats them exactly the same. Their experiences could, nonetheless, be quite different. One employee could view it as more autonomy supportive while the other views it as more controlling, because these two employees came to the situation with different expectations and sensitivities. The first person might see the setting as one that supports choice, so he or she would use relevant information from the situation in making choices, whereas the other person might react to comments as if they were critical and to requests as if they were demands. The former would act more autonomously while the latter would respond either compliantly or defiantly.

In terms of development, experiences that start with different expectations based on past events can result in one person's becoming more autonomous while the other becomes more controlled, even if the two people were in the same context and treated in the same manner. Of course, the context (e.g., their teachers) would probably not treat two such people exactly the same, but I am simply emphasizing that people's preconceived expectations influence how they interpret a social environment and thus can affect whether they are able to rise above it. If a person develops an expectation of autonomy support, which Robert, the school superintendent, may have done from his grandmother and athletic director, the person could fare better in a situation than would others who were there with different expectations.

A child who is born into a home that is both interpersonally and monetarily impoverished faces a far greater set of problems than a child who is born into one that is ripe with supports, but some individuals—today's Abe Lincolns—emerge from these seemingly im-poverished backgrounds to lead exemplary lives. And we now have several pieces of the answer to how this can happen. First, these in-dividuals may have been among the very small percentage of children who are far above the mean on the psychological (and perhaps physi-cal) characteristics that can contribute to developing in healthy, au-tonomous ways. Second, these individuals may have found someone special to give them the interpersonal nutriments they need. Third, they may actually have influenced the cold and controlling adults in their lives to be a little less cold and a little less controlling with them. And, finally, they may have developed expectancies that led them to interpret various situations as more autonomy supportive than they actually were.

While it is true that social environments—whether they be op-pressive or nourishing—have an enormous impact on children's de-velopment, each of the four processes just outlined begins with the individual rather than the environment, and each helps to explain how people can excel in spite of relatively impoverished environ-ments, or, when these processes work in the negative direction, do even worse than would be expected.

Recognizing that our children, students, employees, and patients can affect how we treat them, highlights a very important challenge for us as parents, teachers, managers, and health-care providers. The challenge is to be autonomy supportive even with individuals who pull on us to control them. It is the more passive, compliant, and defiant individuals who are most in need of an optimal interpersonal context—of involvement, autonomy support, and sensitive limit set-ting—but it is these individuals whom we have the hardest time giv-ing it to.

The interactive process between people and their environments continues throughout life. People come to each new situation with their own unique characteristics and interpretations, which have de-veloped in part from past interactions with the environment and which will affect future interactions. These individual differences that people bring to situations allow for some predictability in terms of how the people will respond to the situations, and together with a characterization of the situation itself, they explain a good deal about the interaction between people and their environments.

Individual Differences in Motivation

Richard Ryan and I, with various collaborators, have engaged in a long-term research program to study how individual differences in people's motivation influence their lives. We reason that everyone is to some extent autonomous, and it is that aspect of people that leads them to seek out contexts that are autonomy supportive and to influence others to treat them in a more autonomy-supportive fashion. Similarly, everyone is to some extent controlled (i.e., compliant and/or defiant) in their behavior, and that aspect of them seeks or creates controls. The questions that have interested us concern how individuals' tendency to be autonomous, as opposed to controlled, relates to a wide range of personal characteristics and behaviors.

We began by developing a psychometric instrument to measure the degree to which people are autonomy-oriented and control-oriented, and we have found, for example, that people who are more autonomy-oriented have higher self-esteem and are more self-actualized. They also evidence greater integration in personality. In other words, people who are more autonomous also display greater coherence among various aspects of their personality, as well as between their personality and behavior. Furthermore, people high on the autonomy orientation also have more positive mental health, and report being more satisfied with their interpersonal relationships.

Clearly, then, being autonomy-oriented is associated with positive aspects of personality. Even more interesting, perhaps, are the findings that a strong autonomy orientation leads people to experience social contexts as more autonomy supportive. This, therefore, confirms the point that, through their behavior and expectations, people can influence their environments to provide them with more of what they need.

In one study, for example, patients in a weight-loss program whose personalities were more autonomy-oriented viewed their health-care providers as being more autonomy supportive, and these perceptions, in turn, had positive health consequences. In another study, medical students whose personalities were more autonomy-oriented experienced their instructors as being more autonomy supportive, and that, too, had positive consequences.

The important point, both theoretically and practically, is that the extent to which people's behavior is autonomous, creative, vital, and intrinsically motivated is determined by an interaction of their own personalities (what we call their autonomy orientation) and the degree to which the social context is autonomy supportive. Although the social context is enormously important in affecting people's motivation and behavior, people's personalities also affect their motivation and behavior. What's more, people's personalities also influence the social contexts that, in turn, have an influence on them.

Promoting One's Own Development

The importance of this point is enormous: It gives people a handle to facilitate their own development. True, the environment's influence on people may be greater than they have ever imagined—it works subtly and deeply. True, the environment can undermine people's intrinsic motivation, leaving them passive and compliant without their even realizing it. But by the same token, people *can* change all that. They can begin to act more autonomously. They can figure out what they need for themselves, and they can begin to act on the world to get it.

Rather than waiting for the world to give them what they want, people can become more proactive in making things happen for themselves. They can get the interactive process working on their behalf by behaving more autonomously. They can elicit from the social context more and more support for their autonomy. Their personality and the social contexts in which they operate are synergistic, and together they affect people's experiences and actions.

A few years ago, I consulted to a company in the San Francisco area. The style of the top manager was controlling, and the eight managers who reported to him were quite unhappy. They complained a lot about their manager when I met with each of them individually, but they were very passive and did nothing about it. Not surprisingly, these managers responded to the boss's controlling style by being controlling with their own work teams, so their unhappiness radiated to the one hundred or so people whom they managed. The pattern was a familiar one.

A great deal of my attention while working there was focused on the eight managers. We spent some of the time exploring ways they could be more autonomy supportive with their work teams. But even more important, we worked on ways they could get their *own* needs satisfied. It is eminently clear that if the managers themselves do not feel competent, autonomous, and related to others they will not be autonomy supportive and involved with their subordinates. That, of course, is the same point we confirmed for teachers in the study where they were pressured by the command to be sure their students performed up to high standards. They became more controlling and evaluative of their students—just the opposite of what would have been best for their students and for themselves.

It seemed clear to me that the managers in the Bay Area company had to learn how to use each other—to ask of each other, and to give to each other. And that is what happened. Over the few months that I had periodic meetings with them, I noticed that their office doors were being left open more of the time. They spent more time relating to each other, providing support for each other, and working together to solve problems. They broke through the isolation that had previously characterized the management team. As they began relating to each other differently, providing support for each other, they also became more autonomy supportive with their work teams, leading to a more positive morale in the whole company.

But the change in the way these managers related to their peers and to their subordinates was just part of the overall change that occurred. In addition, they learned how to *manage their manager.* During these few months, the senior manager gained some insight into how demanding and critical he was being with the people who worked for him, and that led to some positive results. But it seemed to me that even more of the positive results were prompted by changes in the team of eight second-level managers. These managers began to deal differently with their boss, and that really made a difference. They asked him for what they needed rather than waiting and sulking as they had done for so long. They began to disagree with him in a polite and constructive way rather than continue to say "Yes, sir" and go away resentfully. They learned to read his moods so they could approach him when there was the best chance of his being responsive. And they learned to give him support, so he would reciprocate.

In one retreat I had with the management team, I encouraged them to give positive feedback to each other, right there in the group meeting. They had a very difficult time at first—not because they couldn't think of anything to say but because they were not used to the process of giving positive feedback within that management team. With practice, it became easier, and part of what they learned about "managing their manager" was that it helped to give him positive feedback.

Over time, the managers discovered that as they became more supportive of their subordinates, their peers, and their boss, those people became more supportive of them. A synergy did indeed develop, and the change in behavior of the eight managers was the thing most responsible for that positive effect. It radiated in both directions, with positive results for the company as a whole.

Managing One's Own Experience

Being autonomous in spite of controlling circumstances is not only about managing the environment. Even more, it is about managing oneself and one's own inner experience. It is about developing the regulatory processes to manage emotions and inner urges and about finding ways to get one's needs satisfied.

Human emotions are a powerful source of energy for action. When angered or frightened, people have an enormous amount of energy. Stories abound about people trapped under an auto or a pile of rubble who are able to extricate themselves. When they feel strong emotions, there is amazing energy available to them. People even report being unable to control themselves when they feel strong emotions.

Establishing the structures and regulatory processes necessary to manage emotions effectively is a major developmental challenge for everyone. Some people have been more successful than others in conquering this challenge, in part certainly, because they had more positive parenting contexts. Those who have succeeded are able to feel their emotions fully while, at the same time, experiencing a genuine choice about how to express them. However, those who have failed to conquer the challenge end up either suppressing their emotions so they don't feel them or being overpowered by their emotions.

I know a man who never seems to feel any emotions, who even when provoked acts as if nothing had happened. He prides himself on being strong. He suppresses his emotions with rigid regulatory structures that he introjected while growing up. He represents quite a contrast with other people I know who always seem to be expressing strong emotions. These people have failed to develop adequate regulatory structures to manage the expression of emotions, so they are frequently overwhelmed by them. Neither case represents optimal regulation of emotions—neither represents autonomous functioning with respect to emotions.

Emotions are reactions to real or imagined stimuli in the current situation or in your memory. A fist coming toward your face, a comment about how nice you look, or a car that pulls out in front of you are all stimuli that can lead to the experience of an emotion. So can the memory of standing on a beach on your honeymoon, or of a time years ago when the class bully called you names and pushed you around.

The stimuli to which people have emotional reactions do not have universal meanings, however. People give their own meanings to the stimuli they encounter, and the meanings given by any two people can be very different. The same stimulus can lead one person to feel joy and another to feel anger because of the unique meaning each gives it. These meanings derive from how the stimulus relates to the people's needs, wants, and expectations.

A friend of mine, Jim Astman, once wrote a song for his younger sister about a time years earlier when she, like most children, had been bothered by monsters. In his song, he counseled her to "make that monster your best friend." The message was simple: Monsters do not frighten you if you do not interpret them as frightening.

Regulating One's Emotions

The process of giving meaning to emotion-eliciting stimuli has two components, as pointed out by psychologist Magda Arnold. When people encounter certain stimuli, they intuit a meaning almost instantaneously, and there is a built-in tendency to respond in certain ways to certain intuited meanings. For example, a fast-moving object that comes hurtling toward the side of your head will almost surely be intuitively experienced as threatening and lead to an immediate surge of adrenaline and the feelings of fright and anger. The tendencies to duck and lash out exist within our nervous system.

But this immediate intuitive responding is only a first step. You then bring a more reflective process to bear, thinking about what is happening. You might realize that the object was not going to hit you but was just a seagull flying past, headed for food that someone had thrown on the ground behind you. Your ability to think deliberately can adjust the immediate interpretation you have given a stimulus, and the emotion you experience will change as the meaning changes. Your fear and anger dissipate as you reappraise what actually happened.

It is the reappraisal process—the more reflective assessment—that gives people power over their emotions, and it was this process that Jim Astman highlighted in his song. The process of giving stimuli less threatening meanings can be a very powerful tool for self-regulation, but unfortunately it is not always easy to accomplish. You have to work at it.

One reason that people interpret many events as threats is that they have developed ego-involvements. Being ego-involved, as was pointed out earlier, means that people's feelings of self-worth are contingent upon some type of outcome. They might have to be seen as intelligent in order to feel worthy, or to be seen as feminine, strong, artistic, or handsome. People can become ego-involved in all sorts of things, and when they are they become highly rigid and controlling with themselves so they will appear intelligent, feminine, or whatever. And when they are ego-involved, they can be easily threatened by others.

Ego-involvements make people a pawn to their emotions. If they need to be seen as strong in order to feel worthy, being called a wimp will threaten their self-worth and could send them into a rage. The anger results from the interpretation of a remark as a threat, but the remark is a threat *only* when people's self-worth is hooked on being seen as strong. People might want to ask themselves, "Is it really that important to be seen as strong (or feminine, or creative, or intelligent, or whatever)?" Is it really worth getting all worked up about and possibly behaving in ways they will later regret? It is interesting to realize that by being ego-involved people give others a weapon. And others quickly learn how to use it.

Nothing is an ego threat if people don't interpret it as such—*if*

they don't threaten their ego with it. Of course, some things are generally more hurtful than others, and an intended insult may be hard
not to interpret as a threat, but people can nonetheless become more
effective at not interpretting stimuli as threats. If there are no realistic
consequences associated with an insult, such as being rejected, abandoned, or fired, people can learn to understand the insult as the
speaker's aggression and not feel so threatened by it, even if it hurts
a little. By learning to interpret stimuli differently, people can
become more effective in managing their own emotions.

Part of how people can rise above the situation is to take interest
in their own ego-involvements, to begin to explore what hooks them.
Then they can ask themselves whether it is really necessary to pressure and control themselves in that way. By exploring their ego-involvements, people can find ways of becoming less reactive, less
controlled, less like a pawn. By exploring their ego-involvements and
how ego-involvements affect the interpretations they give to stimuli,
people can gain the capacity to regulate their own emotions without
suppressing them—people can become more autonomous.

Regulating One's Behavior

Regulating one's emotions by changing the interpretations one gives
to emotion-eliciting stimuli is just one of two essential steps for
becoming more integrated or autonomous with respect to emotions—and in the process, giving oneself a means to rise above controlling forces. The other involves gaining more regulatory flexibility
with respect to the behaviors that one's emotions motivate.

Emotions have certain behavioral tendencies built into them, no
doubt left over from earlier phases in our evolutionary history. These
tendencies—such as striking out when angry, fleeing when frightened, or approaching when joyful—can occur almost automatically,
as an expression of the emotion. But people have the capacity to
inhibit the impulses and decide how to behave.

Becoming autonomous involves developing integrated regulatory processes for managing behavior when emotions have been stimulated. By doing that, people will be able to experience true choice with respect to their behavior when they are angry, disgusted, or joyful. They may choose to talk about it, or not; they may choose to prolong it, or not; they may choose to problem solve, or not; they may simply choose to leave the scene. To the extent that people are integrated with respect to an emotion, they will feel a sense of freedom with respect to how they behave. The emotion will not determine the behavior but instead will be a piece of information relevant to the process of choosing how to behave. Behaviors will be chosen based on an awareness of the emotion and on a consideration of the goals they would like to accomplish. When people are autonomous, they will allow a full experience of their emotions, and they will feel free in deciding how to express them.

In contrast, when emotion-motivated behavior is controlled by introjected regulatory processes, people behave in rigid, programmed ways when a particular emotion is experienced. For example, when people feel anger, an introject might pressure them to get even with those who angered them. "That's how you save face," the introject might say. Or alternatively, it could pressure them to not let others know that they are angry.

Even more extreme, some introjects lead people to suppress their emotions altogether. My acquaintance who never seemed to be bothered by anything provided an example of this. Suppression, however, interferes with natural organismic processes and can have dire consequences. Our emotions are an important messenger. They say to us that we are—or are not—getting something we need. The emotions of fear and anger, for example, can mean that we think we will not get something we expect, desire, or need.

By using emotions as a cue, people can ask themselves two key questions. First, what am I not getting? And, second, do I really need it? Emotions signal a discrepancy between people's current state and some standard they hold. This could mean that it would be useful to find a way to get what they want (for example, more autonomy support from others or more satisfying interpersonal relationships), or it could mean that the expectations or desires they hold are unnecessary or unreasonable. Ego-involvements are an example of standards people hold that may be unnecessary.

Another standard that some people hold that limits their autonomy and experience of life is the belief that all they want in life is to be happy. It is a vague statement, but one that fairy-tale endings are made of. In truth, happiness is not all that it's cracked up to be, and most people don't really want to be happy all the time anyway. People often choose to go to movies or operas that are very unsettling—that terrify, sadden, disgust, or anger them. There is something about experiencing these emotions, whether in the safe and comfortable context of a theater or at a dangerous mountain pass in the Himalayas, that is appealing to many people. They seek a wide range of feelings—the so-called negative as well as the so-called positive. Terror is not happiness. Nor is sadness, disgust, or anger. And it makes no sense to say that feeling anger and disgust makes one happy. Happy is simply the wrong concept for what it is that is natural to people, for what it is that they seek and what it is that promotes human development.

When people want only happiness, they can actually undermine their own development because their quest for happiness can lead them to suppress other aspects of their experience. Wanting to be happy can lead people to avoid (i.e., suppress) sadness when a loved one dies, or to avoid fear in the face of peril. *The true meaning of being alive is not just to feel happy, but to experience the full range of human emotions.* Insofar as the quest for happiness interferes with the experience of other emotions, negative consequences are likely to follow.

Being integrated and autonomous means allowing oneself to feel emotions—all the emotions—and then deciding what to do with them. It is, however, useful to distinguish feelings in terms of the extent to which they are "pure." There are basic emotions that are core to human experience, feelings such as joy, sadness, excitement, and anger, and there are also feelings that have a cognitive overlay. Depression is not a pure emotion. It is often confused with sadness, but the two are quite different. Sadness is pure, and when one feels it, one is nourished by it. Depression is fraught with self-derogation, anxiety, and doubt. Depression is anything but nourishing; it is bewildering and draining. It is maladaptive.

Aggrandizement is similar to depression, in a way. Whereas depression is the result of failure or loss when one has introjected standards, aggrandizement is the result of meeting those standards. Aggrandizement, like depression, is not pure. It has the overlay of boasting about yourself and derogating others. It does not nourish one's true sense of self.

Life is full of a variety of experiences. People succeed, they fail, they build relationships, they lose loved ones. And while one would not typically choose to fail or to lose a loved one, the pure experience of the emotions accompanying these experiences is necessary to make an optimal adjustment to these life changes. Being autonomous involves allowing a full experience of one's emotions, and experiencing emotions can be one of the most gratifying and actualizing elements of being alive. Being autonomous means neither blocking awareness of emotions because of introjected admonitions, nor letting them be overpowering. It means experiencing them fully and feeling a sense of choice about how to express them.

The Use of Techniques

On a recent flight from London, I was served a soft drink by a pleasant, accommodating young flight attendant. He had a rubber band around his right wrist. Jokingly, I said, "nice bracelet," but, actually, I wondered whether he was using it as a behavior modification technique. There is a kind of self-punishment technique in which every time you feel a particular urge or have a certain obsessive thought, you snap the rubber band. It can hurt, and its intent is to break up the thought pattern or overcome the urge by associating it with an unpleasant stimulation.

When it comes to issues of motivation, people always seem to want techniques for motivating or managing themselves. Screaming from the front cover of most self-help books are statements about "The newest techniques for motivating yourself," or "Techniques that have proven effective." The truth is that there are no techniques that will motivate people or make them autonomous. Motivation must come from within, not from techniques. It comes from their deciding they are ready to take responsibility for managing themselves.

When people are really ready to change for their own personal reasons, and when they are willing to face and cope with the myriad feelings—anxiety, inadequacy, rage, terror, or loneliness—that underlie their maladaptive behaviors, then they will have the motivation for change. Once that has happened, various techniques may be useful for them, but without a true resolve, without reasons for change that are personally important, techniques will not help. When people put stock in techniques as something that will change them, they are expressing an external locus of causality rather than an internal one; they are holding the misguided belief that being controlled rather than autonomous is the means for bringing about meaningful, personal change.

A deep personal desire to change must come first. Then perhaps, a technique can give people a little help. I know a man who's a very orderly fellow. He's quite systematic in the way he goes about most things. I remember when he gave up smoking he did it in steps that were all planned out. He had been a two-pack-a-day smoker, and he decided he'd take five months to wean himself. So he set goals: thirty cigarettes a day for the first month; twenty a day for the second; ten a day for the third; five a day for the fourth; and in his last month as a smoker, he said, he'd have two a day—one after lunch and one after dinner. At the end of the fifth month, that would be it, he resolved, and he'd never touch another cigarette. The satisfaction of matching his goal was, he vowed, the only reward he would need. Well, he did it, seven years ago, and he has not had a puff since.

The goal-setting approach suited his character, so that's how he proceeded. It was a useful technique for him. But many people have used the technique and failed miserably. It is not the technique that led the man to stop; it was his autonomous motivation. Some people who have made a resolve to quit will find it easier to go cold turkey, so setting progressively smaller nicotine goals would not be a useful technique for them. Using techniques is likely to be helpful only if it feels right for a person, and only if the person has made a true choice to change. People might try snapping their wrist with a rubber band when they crave a cigarette if that appeals to them. They can buy themselves little presents when they reach standards if that technique seems right for them. They can pick their own technique, if they want to use one at all. But if they are not really ready to change, there is no sense bothering with a technique for it is bound to fail.

Accepting Oneself

The starting place for change is accepting oneself and taking interest in one's inner world. One might wonder, for example: Why do I overeat? Why do I yell at my wife? Why do I spend so little time with my kids? Why am I so dependent on cigarettes? People adopted the behaviors in the first place—perhaps years or even decades earlier—because those behaviors were the best response they could find to deal with a difficult situation.

Discovering the reason they do something can be a helpful start, but it must not be an occasion for blame. Just as the process of change is facilitated by awareness of why people are doing the maladaptive behavior, it is hindered by blaming themselves, or others, for the behavior. When people are truly interested in why they do something, and personally committed to making a change, blame is irrelevant. They might discover that they overeat whenever they feel afraid of failing on some project at work. That's an interesting discovery. And it allows them to figure out how to manage the anxiety in less self-destructive ways. But blaming themselves for overeating or for managing their fear of failure maladaptively will only interfere with lasting change. Remember what Charlotte Selver said: Dare to be fat. Take interest in why you are fat. And then you will be ready to get thin.

A man might discover that he yells at his wife because he does not know how to (or is afraid to) share some of his deep feelings or secrets with her. He yells to keep her at a distance—to protect himself. That, too, is very interesting, and it is the first step in figuring out how to share more of himself, how to open up and be more vulnerable. That may not be easy, but it will likely be more satisfying.

Meaningful change comes out of an organismic readiness. It comes when people feel that now is the time to change, when they are ready to enact a commitment each moment. Pressuring does not help; indeed, it is likely to hurt just as blaming oneself is likely to hurt. When people feel pressured, compliance or defiance results. Compliance produces change that is not likely to be maintained, and defiance blocks change in the first place. Meaningful change occurs when people accept themselves, take interest in why they do what they do, and then decide that they are ready to do differently.

PART FOUR

Conclusion

THIRTEEN

The Meaning of Human Freedom

Garth Fagan is one of the true geniuses in the world of contemporary dance. His troupe has a signature routine in which the dancers soar to unimaginable heights in elegantly original positions. The routine is called "Prelude: Discipline Is Freedom."

The Fagan dancers bound and undulate, with overwhelming energy and force, and yet there is no chaos or anarchy in their work. Rather, there is responsibility and reliance on each other. Every dancer is in precisely the right place at precisely the right time. Quintessential responsibility, but at the same time, amazing freedom and flexibility.

The behavior of these dancers helps illustrate the extremely important point that responsibility need not be felt as obligation, but instead can be associated with freedom. The responsible behavior of these dancers is not controlled, it is autonomous. If the dancers felt pressured to be in the right place—if they had only introjected the necessity of being there—they would not be flexible and free and the marvel of their performance would be lost. But they do act freely, with full volition, so these highly disciplined performers express exceptional creativity.

Abraham Maslow said that "duty is pleasant, and pleasure is the fulfillment of duty." He was making the same point. For him "duty" did not mean obligation or force. It meant giving what the situation asks of you, and giving it freely. If the situation were that your children were hungry, you would feed them. But there is a big difference between doing that out of a sense of love and deeply felt responsibility for your progeny, as opposed to a sense of obligation and duty.

According to the existential philosopher Jean-Paul Sartre, being free means fully accepting one's limitations. Freedom exists within the truth of constraints—not constraints arbitrarily imposed by others, but genuine constraints like those that make us unable to fly, those that make us unable to withstand the force of a tidal wave, and, for some of us, those that make us unable to understand nuclear physics. These are true constraints that exist in the nature of things. But a constraint that gets imposed on a child such as, "Don't make noise or you'll be punished" is not a natural constraint; it is instead arbitrary, imposed by someone in a one-up position. It is shallow compared to the constraints that speak to us about who we really are.

People find freedom in part by accepting their real constraints, but that alone does not ensure that they will function effectively within society. In addition, they may need to accept some of the arbitrary conventions created by the social organization. Society, of course, is very much invested in people's accepting such rules. The important challenge for each individual is to accept the arbitrary constraints that are meaningful to him or her, while at the same time maintaining a sense of personal freedom. The Fagan dancers seem to have done that rather admirably.

While Eastern Europe was still under Soviet domination, I visited many factories, stores, and service agencies in Bulgaria and neighboring countries. I was struck by how little work the employees actually did and by how little they cared about their work. Some told me they frequently went home for three-hour lunch breaks to tend their gardens or do other chores, sometimes making it back to work just in time to sign out for the day. They said they didn't worry because they knew nothing would happen to them. Besides, even if they were to get fired they'd simply get another job. As noted earlier, the communist government essentially guaranteed work and income to all of them, so they were, in an odd sort of way, free to do as they pleased.

Nonetheless, the government imposed many arbitrary constraints and obstacles. People could generally not leave the country, for example, and they had to be extremely careful if they criticized the government. Furthermore, it was typically futile for them to strive for meaningful, personal goals within the system, because bureaucracy and favoritism nearly always determined who would succeed. Individuals were indeed restricted in many ways, but if they did not care about certain behaviors and accomplishments, the system seemed to afford them substantial freedom.

In the West, we hear much about our freedom. It is, in some ways, the mirror image of what I witnessed in Bulgaria that looked like a kind of freedom. In the U.S., people are relatively free from government interference with their mobility, and they have the possibility of accomplishing their personal goals within the system. People can make millions—*if* they are clever enough and willing to work hard enough. They can create a music festival, build a house for themselves, rise in an organizational hierarchy, acquire unlimited possessions, and send their children to the schools they choose—*if* they are able and willing to behave in particular ways. The instrumentalities for accomplishing these goals are relatively clear, and there are relatively few arbitrary restrictions.

However, it is the goals and the necessity of behaving in particular ways that are the kickers. These goals that people are free to pursue can end up controlling the people who pursue them. We saw, for example, in the research by Kasser and Ryan that people who had unusually strong extrinsic aspirations were more controlled and displayed poorer mental health. It is also the case that the necessity to behave in certain ways to achieve an outcome can feel like intense pressure, especially if a person's ego or self-esteem is hinged on the outcome, or if people in one-up positions (like managers and teachers) administer such outcomes in controlling ways.

Ironically, the freedom to pursue one's own ends often results in people relinquishing much of their personal freedom because of their own vulnerabilities—their ego involvements, for example—that developed as their innate psychological needs for competence, autonomy, and relatedness were not adequately satisfied. In our economic system, most people do not feel free to go home during the work day to tend their gardens, because the instrumentalities—the necessity of behaving in particular ways to get desired outcomes—will not allow it. As noted earlier, although these instrumentalities provide information about how to achieve goals, they are also the means through which people can be controlled by their desires and goals, and by the people who administer the instrumentalities.

Were the Bulgarians free when they went home to tend their gardens? Are Americans free when they throw themselves into their work and single-mindedly pursue their goals? To answer these questions, it is necessary to specify exactly what is meant by freedom.

Most frequently, the term freedom is applied at the political or societal level. The people of some societies are said to be free if they are allowed substantial opportunities to choose what to do and how to live, with relatively few arbitrary constraints. In this sense, America is said to allow greater freedom than many other nations, particularly those under totalitarian rule.

Of course, within any society, some may be relatively free and others not, as was the case during the period of slavery within this country. Nonetheless, it is generally possible to characterize societies in terms of how much freedom of action they allow the average citizen to pursue personal goals. The term freedom when used in this way, refers to freedom from external coercion at a systems' level; it refers to minimal government interference in the way you live your life. It means, among other things, not being arbitrarily restricted from living where you want, shopping where you want, traveling where you want, and studying where you want.

At a more proximal level, immediate interpersonal contexts created by people in one-up positions can also limit people's freedom in ways that parallel the limitations created by the broader system. People in one-up positions have authority over others; and they can use that authority in relatively controlling (or alternatively, in relatively autonomy-supportive) ways. Much of the discussion in this book has concerned the way that controlling interpersonal contexts—and elements such as rewards and deadlines contained within them—can limit freedom.

There is, however, yet another way in which people's freedom can be restricted—a way that is even more important to our understanding of human freedom than the distal or proximal controls imposed by social organizations. It is the limitation imposed by inner constraints—by the limitations of our rigid internal structures. I know of a woman who seems to spend all her time talking about the deals she's closed and the money she's made. She is truly driven. She's aggressive and competitive, and making the money and gaining the accompanying influence are apparently more important to her than anything else in her life.

Is she really free? Does she act with a sense of personal freedom as she goes about her daily life? The relative lack of external constraints allows her to pursue her goals. But the obvious strength of the inner pressure to pursue these goals—the degree to which she seems obsessed by them—suggests that she is not an exemplar of personal freedom. And what about the professor who always comes late to meetings? Is he acting freely when he is rebelling against the expectation that he behave like everyone else and be on time?

These two examples—the woman who's building her bank account and the man who is always late—represent lack of personal freedom of two complementary sorts. The first is an instance of compliance with introjected, societally sanctioned values, and the second is an instance of defiance against them. Both are cases of people being restricted, of being compelled by inner forces to act as they do.

From this perspective, *human freedom means to be truly autonomous*. It means to act in a way that is not bounded by introjects, by rigid inner structures, by paralyzing self-criticisms, or by the push to defy limiting forces. To be free means to feel volitional; it means to be governed in one's actions by a true self.

Of course social, political, and economic systems affect the extent to which people are psychologically free. For one thing, systems provide or withhold opportunities to pursue one's goals, and they impose more or fewer arbitrary constraints. But perhaps even more interestingly, social contexts also play a role in creating the internal pressures—the introjected values and regulations—with which people limit their own freedom.

The high value our society places on material accumulation has made people particularly vulnerable to being controlled by contingent financial rewards as well as by contingent love. Thus, when people in one-up positions use these contingencies controllingly, they tend to have clearly negative consequences for the children, students, employees, and patients on whom they are used. As such, people in one-up positions who use rewards controllingly are catalysts for the systemic processes that, in the final analysis, limit the psychological freedom of many people who live within the system. The American system offers substantial freedom to pursue desired outcomes, but paradoxically people's freedom often ends up being limited by the pursuit of these outcomes.

In Bulgaria, employees who left work to go home and tend their gardens could have been free, psychologically, if they had made a true accommodation to the situation. My impression, however, from interviewing many of them, was that very few were free. Most were passive and conflicted. The totalitarian regime had taken a substantial toll even though it had not succeeded in controlling their work behavior. Instead of causing them to commit themselves to their work, it caused their minds to grow sluggish, their arms and legs to grow heavy. Most had relinquished their vitality to the regime because the cost of not doing so seemed too great to bear.

But there were exceptions. One person in particular made a lasting impression on me. He didn't do much work under the communist regime, but instead spent most of his time studying—not at the university because the university was dominated by communist ideology and totalitarian procedures. Rather, he studied foreign languages, Western psychology, capitalist economics, and other such topics. He wrote to scholars in the West requesting articles, and he scoured the university and national libraries for interesting books and articles. Not surprisingly, when President Zhivkov fell from power in 1989 and the country began opening up to the West, this man was ideally suited to be an agent of change.

Social contexts greatly influence the extent to which individuals are free, but they do not determine it. Freedom is a characteristic of an individual's psychological functioning at any given moment. So freedom must be practiced on a moment-to-moment basis. That man in totalitarian Bulgaria had managed to live "freely" a good deal of the time because he had quite successfully freed himself from the oppression of internal controls and conflicts.

Being free does not mean doing your own thing at the expense of others, however. Rather, it involves concern for others and respect for the environment, because those are manifestations of human connectedness. Freedom involves being open to one's inner nature, and there one finds the tendencies for both relatedness and autonomy. Out of the need for relatedness, people grow to respect their social and physical surroundings. The Fagan dancers, while being autonomous in their performing, are also being respectful of the others with whom they perform.

A person who enters a situation and begins immediately to boss people around is not being autonomous because true autonomy is accompanied by relatedness—true autonomy involves respecting others. The person who begins immediately to boss others around is undoubtedly feeling pressured by some internal or external force, and the attempt to control others is simply a manifestation of that pressure. Were the person autonomous, he or she would begin by accepting the environment before immediately trying to change it.

I have a friend, a very active and assertive man, who walks into any situation and begins to change things—more light, less air, more pepper, less noise, move that table, hide the pillow. He seems to keep everything in motion. In a way, I respect the fact that he gets what he needs for himself, but I've always felt that it was too much. It's not really autonomy and freedom being exhibited—it's too pressured. It is as if he always had to prove something. I want to say, "Take it easy. Feel out the situation. Respect what is here. Be sensitive to others. And then maybe think about changing it."

True freedom involves a balance between being proactive in dealing with one's environment and being respectful of it. Being psychologically free entails an attitude of accepting others. We are not ends in ourselves but part of a larger system, and because the true self has the dual tendencies toward autonomy and relatedness, the person who acts from a well-developed self will accept others and will respect the environment, as well as proactively influencing both.

H uman freedom leads to authenticity; it is about being who we truly are. And with freedom comes responsibility, because that is part of who we truly are. It is in our nature to develop responsibly, as we strive to become integrated with the social community. What psychologist Andras Angyal called our "homonomous tendency" (i.e., our tendency to be in union with a larger unit), in combination with our "autonomous tendency," urges us toward responsibility. Actualizing those tendencies (and thus achieving integration and well-being), however, requires nutriments from the socializing context. Society influences people's psychological freedom in accord with whether it (and the socializing agents who are its representatives) provides or withholds those nutriments.

Unfortunately, the concepts of freedom, authenticity, and responsibility have been so badly misportrayed by social critics over the past few decades that the issues surrounding these concepts have become hopelessly muddled. Because current research on human autonomy provides a basis for clarifying the muddle and explicating the meaning of human freedom, let us briefly use that work to reflect on developments of the past few decades that have been debated by social critics.

The 1960s was a tense and dramatic decade. A wide-ranging social movement gained substantial momentum as people like the funny and truculent Abbie Hoffman, followed by millions of the country's youth, took rebellion to the center of the national stage. Some, like Abbie, were angry souls who rebelled against all forms of structure—"revolution for the hell of it," he said—and some were lost souls who mimicked their rebellious leaders in a desperate attempt to belong. Together they marched, the angry and the lost, side-by-side. At times they broke windows, burned buildings, and even robbed banks. They called for authenticity and social responsibility, but they lacked these very characteristics in their own lives.

But the sixties was a complex time. Neither rebellion nor control was the essence of that period for some of the people living through it. Instead, these people were concerned with the compelling themes of the period—the themes of finding their own truth, loving one another, valuing the earth, questioning whether war is necessary, and developing greater personal and social responsibility. These people had taken the messages to heart and were working to be authentic in their own lives. These were the people who were enriched by the movement.

Social critics who have reflected on this period have generally portrayed it as either good or bad, because they have focused only on those who were authentically searching or only on those who were irresponsibly rebelling. Charles Reich saw it as part of an essential revolution that would yield more authentic individuals and a more human community, but Christopher Lasch labeled it a time of narcissistic self-gratification. Psychologist Rollo May said that the sixties movement was about discovering oneself through love and will, but writer James Lincoln Collier said it was a movement that promoted self-indulgence as a virtue. By failing to recognize the diversity of purpose, each of these writers failed to grasp one of the most important issues of our time, namely how people can be both *authentic* and *responsible* in a society whose values and systems seem to thwart those goals at every turn.

Part of the problem was that the polarized feelings of that troubled period led writers to give perverse meanings to terms. Allan Bloom essentially portrayed authenticity and self-indulgence as the same thing, asserting that to be authentic means to care for yourself instead of for others. He thus implied, incorrectly, that a self-affirming autonomy and a deep sense of personal responsibility could not coexist in the same individual.

It is true that much of the rebellion of the period was irresponsible and indulgent, and to that extent it was not authentic. It was instead a response to introjected rigidities that had created in people an "inner voice" that sounded much like the voice of their elders. This swallowed voice of control, which was intended to make society's youngsters fall into line with society's ideals, pressured and demanded, evaluated and criticized. And the dominant response to these controls, which was compliance during the fifties, became defiance during the sixties.

By the eighties, compliance had once again ascended and was hailed by many as a virtue. The conformity and achievement of those who looked disciplined—who acted right, dressed right, talked right, and fit right in—were handsomely rewarded. I encountered hundreds of compliant students during the eighties. They had stepped on the treadmill and were headed for Wall Street or Madison Avenue. Young men dressed in polo shirts with tasteful gold chains and designer jeans; young women even wore skirts to class. They sought success, and they selected courses and extracurricular activities that would look good on their résumés. These were the children of the eighties for whom the controls had worked to promote compliance in a world where writer Ayn Rand and economist Milton Friedman were the prophets.

These students supported the Gulf War with the same vigor that students of the sixties opposed the Vietnam War, and they did so with rhetoric rather than reason, just as many of the anti-Vietnam activists had. I remember one well-dressed, pleasant young man who started in on the Gulf War after class one day. He went on and on about patriotism, about Saddam being another Hitler, about stopping imperial aggression. I simply nodded.

An interesting parallel can be found between the students of the sixties and the students of the eighties. In the sixties, some defied and rebelled while others worked to be authentic and responsible, whereas in the eighties some complied and manipulated while others worked to be authentic and responsible. Those who complied in the eighties were as irresponsible as those who rebelled in the sixties, for neither were acting freely on the basis of integrated values.

When controls of society are merely introjected by people, those people may either comply or defy. But neither compliance nor defiance represents authenticity, and neither represents responsibility. To defy what authority says just because authority says it, is to be irresponsible. But in a quite profound sense, it is also true that to comply with authority just because it is authority is to be irresponsible.

Responsibility—true responsibility—requires that people act autonomously in relating to the world around, that they behave authentically on behalf of some general good. In each epoch—the sixties and the eighties—there were caring and committed students who toiled on behalf of the homeless, the neglected, and the victims of violence. They behaved responsibly as a manifestation of their authenticity—of their being in contact with their own inner selves and with the inner selves of others. They were responsible because they were able to unhook themselves from the controls around them, because they were able to avoid the dynamics of compliance and defiance.

As we proceed through the nineties, the dynamics of the earlier periods seem to have become amplified in response to social contexts that are either overly controlling or permissive. Pressures are mounting, and people are responding in a variety of irresponsible ways. And as they do, the calls for greater control can be heard all around—from critics, from politicians, from average citizens, from countless people who themselves are behaving irresponsibly. The problem, of course, is that more control will only make things worse.

A t the heart of human freedom is the experience of choice. When autonomous, people experience choice about how to behave, but when controlled (whether they comply or defy), they experience a lack of choice. If someone held a gun to your head and said, "Jump," you would likely jump, experiencing no choice about it. So, too, if an introject said jump, you might also jump and experience no choice. Such forces, whether external or internal, diminish people's experience of choice, and they have very significant consequences for the quality of people's behavior and well-being.

Existential philosophers would say that people always have choice. According to Sartre, for example, at each moment, people create their existence with their choices, and they are thus fully responsible for themselves. However, although in a sense that is true, and although it is the capacity to choose even in a pressured world that allows people to rise above political and economic influences, there is another sense in which the assertion that people always have choice fails to convey the nature of human experience. As living organisms, people have vulnerabilities, and these vulnerabilities make it incredibly difficult to maintain a sense of freedom and health in the face of an aggressive lack of support for their basic human needs. To maintain a sense of freedom and authenticity when one is starving and food is made dependent on caving in would be a relatively superhuman feat. In a sense, one would be choosing to sell one's integrity for food and water, but that is so only in a rather abstract sense, for it fails to give adequate consideration to the experience of coercion and the human needs that are integral to the episode.

At the same time that the truth of human vulnerabilities is apparent, and can substantially limit human freedom, the existential position presents each of us with an important challenge. It says to us that we are indeed responsible for ourselves, and it challenges us to accept that responsibility rather than giving in to the forces of chaos and control.

In December 1985, Elena Bonner, Soviet dissident and wife of physicist/activist Andrei Sakharov, was allowed to leave her house arrest in the USSR to seek medical attention in the West. She spent six months undergoing surgery, visiting her mother and her children, and writing a memoir before she returned to her life of imprisonment.

The Sakharovs, who had lived in internal exile for several years, were under the constant watch of the KGB, had no access to a phone, and were allowed almost no opportunity to leave their apartment unaccompanied by guards. They went on hunger strikes, were accused of numerous crimes against the state, and were arbitrarily accosted by authorities. All manner of controls were applied to the Sakharovs—forced injections of nutriments during their hunger strikes, constant break-ins at their apartment, accusations, harassment, and intimidation—and the Sakharovs stood their ground. They acted from their consciences, they spoke their beliefs, they refused to be broken.

Bonner could probably have stayed in the U.S. as a defector, and part of her no doubt wanted to. Most of her family was here, and she had myriad opportunities that must surely have appealed to her. The Western system offered her substantial freedom of action, but she accepted the existential challenge and chose to return to her life of internal exile. Why? Because Sakharov was there waiting. She could have remained in a land that provides a certain kind of political freedom, but instead she chose to subject herself to one of the most hideous forms of oppression. She chose it because sharing life's experiences with her husband was the most important thing to her.

Elena Bonner was being autonomous; her decision came from what we call an integrated sense of self. It was a true choice, an action not controlled by introjects or other pressures. As Bonner put it, "together . . . we are still free to be ourselves." In a system of political control, the Sakharovs displayed greater personal freedom than do millions of people whose governments do not oppress them politically.

NOTES ON
WORKS CITED

CHAPTER ONE

Charles A. Reich. *The Greening of America*. New York: Random House, 1970.

Christopher Lasch. *The Culture of Narcissism*. New York: Norton, 1978.

Allan Bloom. *The Closing of the American Mind*. New York: Simon and Schuster, 1987.

Loren Baritz. *The Good Life*. New York: Knopf, 1988.

Donald Winnicott. *Human Nature*. New York: Schocken, 1986.

Alice Miller. *The Drama of the Gifted Child: The Search for the True Self* (R. Ward, Trans.). New York: Basic Books, 1981.

CHAPTER TWO

Harry F. Harlow. Motivation as a factor in the acquisition of new responses. In *Current theory and research on motivation* (pp. 24–49). Lincoln, NB: University of Nebraska Press, 1953.

B. F. Skinner. *Science and Human Behavior*. New York: Macmillan, 1953.

Barry Schwartz. *The Battle for Human Nature*. New York: Norton, 1986.

Robert Henri quoted in Robert Goldwater and Marco Trever, *Artists on Art*. New York: Pantheon, 1945. P. 401.

Richard deCharms. *Personal Causation: The Internal Affective Determinants of Behavior*. New York: Academic Press, 1968.

Charles Reich. *The Greening of America*. New York: Random House, 1970.

CHAPTER THREE

Henry A. Murray. *Explorations in Personality*. New York: Oxford University Press, 1938.

CHAPTER FOUR

Mihaly Csikszentmihalyi. *Flow*. New York: Harper, 1990.

Charles Taylor. *The Ethics of Authenticity*. Cambridge, MA: Harvard University Press, 1992.

Teresa M. Amabile. *The Social Psychology of Creativity*. New York: Springer-Verlag, 1983.

Frederick W. Taylor. *Principles of Scientific Management*. New York: Harper, 1911.

CHAPTER FIVE

Henry K. H. Woo. *The Unseen Dimensions of Wealth*. Fremont, CA: Victoria Press, 1984.

James P. Connell. Context, self and action: A motivational analysis of self-system processes across the life-span. In D. Cicchetti & M. Beeghly (Eds.), *The Self in Transition: Infancy to Childhood* (pp. 61–97). Chicago: University of Chicago Press, 1990.

Ellen A. Skinner. *Perceived Control, Motivation, and Coping*. Newbury Park, CA: Sage, 1995.

R. W. White. Motivation reconsidered: The concept of competence. *Psychological Review*, 1959, 66, 297–333.

Albert Bandura. *Social Foundations of Thought and Action: A Social Cognitive Theory*. Englewood Cliffs, NJ: Prentice-Hall, 1986.

CHAPTER SIX

Sigmund Freud. *The Ego and the Id*. New York: Norton, 1962. (Original work published 1923.)

Carl Rogers. *Client-centered therapy*. Boston: Houghton-Mifflin, 1951.

Frederick S. Perls. *Gestalt Therapy Verbatim*. Lafayette, CA: Real People Press, 1969.

B. F. Skinner. *About Behaviorism*. New York: Knopf, 1974.

Jean Piaget. *Biology and Knowledge*. Chicago: University of Chicago Press, 1971.

Talcott Parsons. *The Social System.* Glencoe, IL: The Free Press, 1951.
Abraham H. Maslow. *Motivation and Personality.* New York: Harper & Row, 1954.

CHAPTER SEVEN

Fritz Perls. *The Gestalt Approach and Eyewitness to Therapy.* Ben Lomond, CA: Science and Behavior Books, 1973.

CHAPTER EIGHT

Alice Miller. *The Drama of the Gifted Child: The Search for the True Self* (R. Ward, Trans.). New York: Basic Books, 1981.
Charles V. W. Brooks. *Sensory Awareness: The Rediscovery of Experiencing Through Workshops with Charlotte Selver.* Great Neck, NY: Felix Morrow, 1986.
Elie Wiesel. *Night* (Stella Rodway, trans.). New York: Hill & Wang, 1960.
Erich Fromm. *The Art of Loving.* New York: Harper & Row, 1956.

CHAPTER NINE

Charles A. Reich. *The Greening of America.* New York: Random House, 1970.
Paul Wachtel. *The Poverty of Affluence: A Psychological Portrait of the American Way of Life.* New York: Free Press, 1983.
James Patterson & Peter Kim. *The Day America Told the Truth.* New York: Prentice-Hall, 1991.
Ayn Rand. *The Virtue of Selfishness.* New York: The New American Library, 1961.
Carol Gilligan. *In a Different Voice.* Cambridge, MA: Harvard University Press, 1982.
Robert Young. *Personal Autonomy: Beyond Negative and Positive Liberty.* New York: St. Martin's Press, 1986.

CHAPTER TEN

A. S. Neill. *Summerhill: A Radical Approach to Child Rearing.* New York: Hart, 1960.
E. C. Tolman. *Purposive Behavior in Animals and Men.* New York: Century, 1932.

K. Lewin. *The Conceptual Representation and Measurement of Psychological Forces*. Durham, NC: Duke University Press, 1938.

CHAPTER ELEVEN

J. M. McGinnis & W. H. Foege. Actual causes of death in the United States. *Journal of the American Medical Association,* 1993, *270*(18), 2207–2212.
Hans Selye. *The Stress of Life* (2nd edition). New York: McGraw-Hill, 1975.

CHAPTER TWELVE

Magda Arnold. *Emotion and Personality, Vol. 1: Psychological Aspects.* New York: Columbia University Press, 1960.

CHAPTER THIRTEEN

Abraham Maslow. *Toward a Psychology of Being.* Princeton, NJ: Van Nostrand, 1962.
Jean-Paul Sartre. *Critique of Dialectical Reason.* New York: Verso, 1991.
Andras Angyal. *Neurosis and Treatment: A Holistic Theory.* New York: Wiley, 1965.
Charles Reich. *The Greening of America.* New York: Random House, 1970.
Christopher Lasch. *The Culture of Narcissism.* New York: Norton, 1978.
Rollo May. *Love and Will.* New York: Norton, 1969.
James Lincoln Collier. *The Rise of Selfishness in America.* New York: Oxford University Press, 1990.
Ayn Rand. *The Fountainhead.* Indianapolis: Bobbs-Merrill, 1943.
Milton Friedman. *Why Government Is the Problem.* Stanford, CA: Hoover Institute on War, Revolution, and Peace, Stanford University, 1993.
Jean-Paul Sartre. *Existentialism and Human Emotions.* New York: Philosophical Library, 1957.
Elena Bonner. *Alone Together.* New York: Knopf, 1986.

LIST OF
RESEARCH ARTICLES

Amabile, T. M., DeJong, W., & Lepper, M. R. (1976). Effects of externally imposed deadlines on subsequent intrinsic motivation. *Journal of Personality and Social Psychology, 34,* 92–98.

Benware, C., & Deci, E. L. (1975). Attitude change as a function of the inducement for espousing a pro-attitudinal communication. *Journal of Experimental Social Psychology, 11,* 271–278.

Benware, C., & Deci, E. L. (1984). The quality of learning with an active versus passive motivational set. *American Educational Research Journal, 21,* 755–766.

Blais, M. R., Sabourin S., Boucher, C., & Vallerand, R. J. (1990). Toward a motivational model of couple happiness. *Journal of Personality and Social Psychology, 59,* 1021–1031.

Boggiano, A. K. & Barrett, M. (1985). Performance and motivational deficits of helplessness: The role of motivational orientations. *Journal of Personality and Social Psychology, 49,* 1753–1761.

Boggiano, A. K. & Ruble, D. N. (1979). Competence and the overjustification effect: A developmental study. *Journal of Personality and Social Psychology, 37,* 1462–1468.

Danner, F. W. & Lonky, E. (1981). A cognitive-developmental approach to the effects of rewards on intrinsic motivation. *Child Development, 52,* 1043–1052.

Deci, E. L. (1971). Effects of externally mediated rewards on intrinsic motivation. *Journal of Personality and Social Psychology, 18,* 105–115.

Deci, E. L. (1972). Intrinsic motivation, extrinsic reinforcement, and inequity. *Journal of Personality and Social Psychology, 22,* 113–120.

Deci, E. L. (1972). The effects of contingent and non-contingent rewards and controls on intrinsic motivation. *Organizational Behavior and Human Performance, 8,* 217–229.

Deci, E. L., Betley, G., Kahle, J., Abrams, L., & Porac, J. (1981). When trying to win: Competition and intrinsic motivation. *Personality and Social Psychology Bulletin, 7,* 79–83.

Deci, E. L., & Cascio, W. F. (1972, April). Changes in intrinsic motivation as a function of negative feedback and threats. Eastern Psychological Association, Boston, MA.

Deci, E. L., Cascio, W. F., & Krusell, J. (1975). Cognitive evaluation theory and some comments on the Calder and Staw critique. *Journal of Personality and Social Psychology, 31,* 81–85.

Deci, E. L., Connell, J. P., & Ryan, R. M. (1989). Self-determination in a work organization. *Journal of Applied Psychology, 74,* 580–590.

Deci, E. L., Driver, R. E., Hotchkiss, L., Robbins, R. J., & Wilson, I. M. (1993). The relation of mothers' controlling vocalizations to children's intrinsic motivation. *Journal of Experimental Child Psychology, 55,* 151–162.

Deci, E. L., Eghrari, H., Patrick, B. C., Leone, D. (1994). Facilitating internalization: The self-determination theory perspective. *Journal of Personality, 62,* 119–142.

Deci, E. L., Hodges, R., Pierson, L., & Tomassone, J. (1992). Autonomy and competence as motivational factors in students with learning disabilities and emotional handicaps. *Journal of Learning Disabilities, 25,* 457–471.

Deci, E. L., Nezlek, J., & Sheinman, L. (1981). Characteristics of the rewarder and intrinsic motivation of the rewardee. *Journal of Personality and Social Psychology, 40,* 1–10.

Deci, E. L., & Ryan, R. M. (1985). The general causality orientations scale: Self-determination in personality. *Journal of Research in Personality, 19,* 109–134.

Deci, E. L., & Ryan, R. M. (1993). Die Selbstbestimmungstheorie der Motivation und ihre Bedeutung für die Pädagogik. *Zeitschrift für Pädagogik, 39,* 223–238.

Deci, E. L., Schwartz, A. J., Sheinman, L., & Ryan, R. M. (1981). An instrument to assess adults' orientations toward control versus autonomy with children: Reflections on intrinsic motivation and perceived competence. *Journal of Educational Psychology, 73,* 642–650.

Deci, E. L., Speigel, N. H., Ryan, R. M., Koestner, R., & Kauffman, M. (1982). The effects of performance standards on teaching styles: The behavior of controlling teachers. *Journal of Educational Psychology,* 74, 852–859.

Enzle, M. E., & Anderson S. C. (1993). Surveillant intentions and intrinsic motivation. *Journal of Personality and Social Psychology, 64,* 257–266.

Frederick, C. M., & Ryan, R. M. (1993). Differences in motivation for sport and exercise and their relations with participation and mental health. *Journal of Sport Behavior, 16,* 124–146.

Grolnick, W. S. & Ryan, R. M. (1987). Autonomy in children's learning: An experimental and individual difference investigation. *Journal of Personality and Social Psychology, 52,* 890–898.

Grolnick, W. S. & Ryan, R. M. (1989). Parent styles associated with children's self-regulation and competence in school. *Journal of Educational Psychology, 81,* 143–154.

Grolnick, W. S., Ryan, R. M., & Deci, E. L. (1991). The inner resources for school performance: Motivational mediators of children's perceptions of their parents. *Journal of Educational Psychology, 83,* 508–517.

Harackiewicz, J. (1979). The effects of reward contingency and performance feedback on intrinsic motivation. *Journal of Personality and Social Psychology, 37,* 1352–1363.

Harackiewicz, J. M., Sansone, C., Blair, L. W., Epstein, J. A., & Manderlink, G. (1987). Attributional processes in behavior change and maintenance: Smoking cessation and continued abstinence. *Journal of Consulting and Clinical Psychology, 55,* 372–378.

Ilardi, B. C., Leone, D., Kasser, R., & Ryan, R. M. (1993). Employee and supervisor ratings of motivation: Main effects and discrepancies associated with job satisfaction and adjustment in a factory setting. *Journal of Applied Social Psychology, 23,* 1789–1805.

Kage, M. (1991, September). *The effects of evaluation on intrinsic motivation.* Paper presented at the meetings of the Japan Association of Educational Psychology, Joetsu, Japan.

Kasser, T., & Ryan, R. M. (1993). A dark side of the American dream: Correlates of financial success as a central life aspiration. *Journal of Personality and Social Psychology, 65,* 410–422.

Kasser, T., & Ryan, R. M. (in press). Further examining the American dream: The differential effects of intrinsic and extrinsic goal structures. *Personality and Social Psychology Bulletin.*

Kasser, T., Ryan, R. M., Zax, M., & Sameroff, A. J. (in press). The relations of maternal and social environments to late adolescents' materialistic and prosocial aspirations. *Developmental Psychology.*

Kast, A. D. (1988). Sex and age differences in response to informational and controlling feedback. *Personality and Social Psychology Bulletin, 14,* 514–523.

Koestner, R., Ryan, R. M., Bernieri, F., & Holt, K. (1984). Setting limits on children's behavior: The differential effects of controlling versus informational styles on children's intrinsic motivation and creativity. *Journal of Personality, 54,* 233–248.

Lepper, M. R. & Greene, D. (1975). Turning play into work: Effects of adult surveillance and extrinsic rewards on children's intrinsic motivation. *Journal of Personality and Social Psychology, 31,* 479–486.

Lepper, M. R., Greene, D., & Nisbett, R. E. (1973). Undermining children's intrinsic interest with extrinsic rewards: A test of the "overjustification" hypothesis. *Journal of Personality and Social Psychology, 28,* 129–137.

Manderlink, G. & Harackiewicz, J. M. (1984). Proximal vs. distal goal setting and intrinsic motivation. *Journal of Personality and Social Psychology, 47,* 918–928.

McGraw, K. O. (1978). The detrimental effects of reward on performance: A literature review and a prediction model. In M. R. Lepper & D. Greene (Eds.), *The hidden costs of reward* (pp. 33–60). Hillsdale, NJ: Erlbaum.

Mossholder, K. W. (1980). Effects of externally mediated goal setting on intrinsic motivation: A laboratory experiment. *Journal of Applied Psychology, 65,* 202–210.

Plant, R. W. & Ryan, R. M. (1985). Intrinsic motivation and the effects of self-consciousness, self-awareness, and ego-involvement: An investigation of internally controlling styles. *Journal of Personality, 53,* 435–449.

Reeve, J., & Deci, E. L. (in press). Elements within the competitive situation that affect intrinsic motivation. *Personality and Social Psychology Bulletin.*

Ross, M. (1975). Salience of reward and intrinsic motivation. *Journal of Personality and Social Psychology, 32,* 245–254.

Ryan, R. M. (1982). Control and information in the intrapersonal sphere: An extension of cognitive evaluation theory. *Journal of Personality and Social Psychology, 43,* 450–461.

Ryan, R. M., & Connell, J. P. (1989). Perceived locus of causality and internalization: Examining reasons for acting in two domains. *Journal of Personality and Social Psychology, 57,* 749–761.

Ryan, R. M., Connell, J. P., & Plant, R. W. (1990). Emotions in non-directed text learning. *Learning and Individual Differences, 2,* 1–17.

Ryan, R. M., & Frederick, C. M. (1994). Psychological vitality: A theory and construct. Unpublished manuscript, University of Rochester.

Ryan, R. M. & Grolnick, W. S. (1986). Origins and pawns in the classroom: Self-report and projective assessments of children's perceptions. *Journal of Personality and Social Psychology, 50,* 550–558.

Ryan, R. M., Koestner, R., & Deci, E. L. (1991). Varied forms of persistence: When free-choice behavior is not intrinsically motivated. *Motivation and Emotion, 15,* 185–205.

Ryan, R. M., & Lynch, J. (1989). Emotional autonomy versus detachment: Revisiting the vicissitudes of adolescence and young adulthood. *Child Development, 60,* 340–356.

Ryan, R. M., Mims, V., & Koestner, R. (1983). Relation of reward contingency and interpersonal context to intrinsic motivation: A review and test using cognitive evaluation theory. *Journal of Personality and Social Psychology, 45,* 736–750.

Ryan, R. M., Plant, R. W., & O'Malley, S. (in press). Initial motivations for alcohol treatment: Relations with patient characteristics, treatment involvement, and dropout. *Addictive Behaviors.*

Ryan, R. M., Rigby, S., & King, K. (1993). Two types of religious internalization and their relations to religious orientation and mental health. *Journal of Personality and Social Psychology, 65,* 586–596.

Ryan, R. M., Stiller, J., & Lynch, J. H. (1994). Representations of relationships to teachers, parents, and friends as predictors of academic motivation and self-esteem. *Journal of Early Adolescence, 14,* 226–249.

Ryan, R. M., Vallerand, R., & Deci, E. L. (1984). Intrinsic motivation in sport: A cognitive evaluation theory interpretation. In W. F. Straub & J. M. Williams (Eds.), *Cognitive sport psychology,* pp. 231–241. Lansing, NY: Sport Science Associates.

Sheldon, K. M., Ryan, R. M., Reis, H. T., & Rigby, S. (1994). What makes for a good day? Competence and autonomy in the day and in the person. Unpublished manuscript, University of Rochester.

Smith, W. E. (1974). *The effects of social and monetary rewards on intrinsic motivation.* Unpublished doctoral dissertation, Cornell University.

Strauss, J. & Ryan, R. M. (1987). Autonomy disturbances in anorexia nervosa. *Journal of Abnormal Psychology, 96,* 254–258.

Swann, W. B. & Pittman, T. S. (1977). Initiating play activity of children: The moderating influence of verbal cues on intrinsic motivation. *Child Development, 48,* 1128–1132.

Vallerand, R. J., & Bissonnette, R. (1992). Intrinsic, extrinsic, and amotivational styles as predictors of behavior: A prospective study. *Journal of Personality, 60,* 599–620.

Vallerand, R. J., Blais, M. R., Lacouture, Y., & Deci, E. L. (1987). L'Echelle des orientations générales à la causalité: Validation Canadienne Française du General Causality Orientations Scale. *Canadian Journal of Behavioral Science, 19,* 1–15.

Williams, G. C., & Deci, E. L. (1995). Internalization of biopsychosocial values by medical students: A test of self-determination theory. Unpublished manuscript, University of Rochester.

Williams, G. C., Grow, V. M., Freedman, Z. R., Ryan, R. M., & Deci, E. L. (1995). Motivational predictors of weight loss and weight-loss maintenance. Unpublished manuscript, University of Rochester.

Williams, G. C., Quill, T. E., Deci, E. L., & Ryan, R. M. (1991). The facts concerning the recent carnival of smoking in Connecticut (and elsewhere). *Annals of Internal Medicine, 115,* 59–63.

Williams, G. C., Rodin, G. C., Ryan, R. M., Grolnick, W. S., & Deci, E. L. (1994). Compliance or autonomous regulation: New insights about medication taking from understanding human motivation. Unpublished manuscript, University of Rochester.

Williams, G. C., Wiener, M. W., Markakis, K. M., Reeve, J., & Deci, E. L. (1994). Medical student motivation for internal medicine. *Journal of General Internal Medicine, 9,* 327–333.

Zuckerman, M., Porac, J. F., Lathin, D., Smith, R., & Deci, E. L. (1978). On the importance of self-determination for intrinsically motivated behavior. *Personality and Social Psychology Bulletin, 4,* 443–446.

INDEX